James Liddy

On American Literature and Diasporas

Eamonn Wall
EDITOR

James Liddy

ON AMERICAN LITERATURE AND DIASPORAS

ARLEN
HOUSE

ON AMERICAN LITERATURE AND DIASPORAS

is published in 2013 by
ARLEN HOUSE
42 Grange Abbey Road
Baldoyle
Dublin 13
Ireland
Phone/Fax: 353 86 8207617
Email: arlenhouse@gmail.com

Distributed internationally by
SYRACUSE UNIVERSITY PRESS
621 Skytop Road, Suite 110
Syracuse, NY 13244–5290
Phone: 315–443–5534/Fax: 315–443–5545
Email: supress@syr.edu

ISBN 978–1–85132–044–8, paperback
ISBN 978–1–85132–054–7, hardback

Typesetting ¦ Arlen House
Printing ¦ Brunswick Press

Contents

Eamonn Wall

INTRODUCTION

As James Liddy recalls in "A Salute to the Good: My University Life," the opening essay in this volume, he arrived in the United States on 11 September 1967, to take up a one-year visiting professor position at San Francisco State University. He was not alone among Irish poets of his generation in setting out for America: John Montague, Thomas Kinsella, Derek Mahon, Seamus Heaney, Eamon Grennan, Paul Muldoon and Eavan Boland, among poets we might list as being his near or close contemporaries, have also lived for extended periods in the United States. Of equal importance, though receiving less attention, have been the journeys made to Ireland by such American poets as Robinson Jeffers, Sylvia Plath, Theodore Roethke, Jean Valentine, Anne Kennedy, Ted McNulty, John Berryman and others. Famously, Berryman came to Dublin to complete his *Dream Songs,* one of the great works of contemporary American poetry, and to contend with the great shadow cast by Yeats, "I have moved to Dublin to have it out with you, /majestic Shade" (334). Irish poets making the reverse journey go partly to address their own great American Shades: we observe Montague is in dialogue with Williams and Rexroth; Muldoon with Frost; Boland with Levertov and Rich; Liddy with Spicer and Niedecker.

Since the days of the Irish Literary Revival, Irish and American poets have always given attention to what is being written on the opposite side of the Atlantic. Continuously, the Irish and American literary communities, forming vibrant, original, hyper, noisy and creative spaces at the margins of traditional English Literature, have sought each other out. Along with Montague and Boland, Liddy shares a closer connection to America than most Irish poets. Montague was born and spent part of his childhood in Brooklyn; Boland lived a part of her adolescence in New York; Liddy was raised in Co. Wexford by his dispensary doctor father, who had trained at the Mayo Clinic in Minnesota, and his American born-and-raised mother. At a deep level perhaps, Liddy's journey to America, away from Ireland, was a journey home to his second motherland. Given his singular personal history, it is not surprising that James Liddy did not consider himself to be an immigrant in the traditional sense. Also, his own particular status allowed for a unique literary perspective: though he was passionately attached to both Ireland and America – places and literary communities – he was better able than most to separate himself from the mythologies that enveloped both. Underlying Liddy's work, in all genres, are contending waves of passionate belonging and fierce skepticism. As a writer his work is engaged, fierce and honest with the result that, as readers, we are forced to realign our gazes as we face new truths and brighter conclusions.

Liddy's fascination with American literature predated his arrival in America. In "The Architects of Love: Patrick Kavanagh and the Beat Generation," he recalls the excitement of buying City Lights books in Hodges Figgis in Dublin during the sixties and absorbing from them new literary attitudes and forms brought into view by Allen Ginsberg, Gregory Corso, and others. His arrival in the United States allowed him to engage with American writing more deeply, to read the work of writers whose books had not made their way to Ireland, and to experience the country and peoples of America first-hand. Also, by living abroad he was able to refine his understanding of Ireland and its literature, "one advantage of abroad, overseas, is to be able to play with the matter of Ireland. You can camp it up or at the very least force it into unfamiliar patterns," as he noted in a short essay written for *Metre*. Of course, long holidays and sabbaticals made it possible for Liddy to retain an Irish footprint: for many years, he spent a month or two in the family home in Coolgreany, Co. Wexford, where he renewed his ties to the local community. He remained in touch with many in the Irish literary world whom he would meet on his forays into Dublin. A member of Aosdána whose work continued to appear under the imprint of Irish publishers, Salmon Poetry and Arlen House in particular, and a reviewer for *The Irish Times*, James Liddy continued to occupy a noticeable place in the Irish literary world. He also traveled widely throughout America, published his work in American literary journals and magazines, gave many readings and lectures, and maintained enduring friendships with many American poets.

As a young writer in Dublin in the decade before his departure, James Liddy had been part of the literary and bohemian world that formed a circle around the poet Patrick Kavanagh and was centered on McDaid's of Harry St, just off Grafton St., Dublin. It was in these complex environs, so wonderfully detailed in Anthony Cronin's *Dead as Doornails* and John Ryan's *Remembering How We Stood* that Liddy grew as a poet publishing his first collections of poetry, *In a Blue Smoke* and *Blue Mountain* with Dolmen Press in 1964 and 1968, respectively. With Liam O'Connor and Michael Hartnett, he edited *Arena*, four issues appearing between 1963–65, in which many of Kavanagh's last poems were published as well as the work of young writers who were making their first entries into publication: John McGahern, Christy Brown and Derek Mahon to name but three of the more prominent.

When his visiting position ended at San Francisco State, Liddy moved on to various other short-term academic jobs in American and Irish universities: the State University of New York at Binghamton; Lewis & Clark College, Oregon; Denison University, Ohio; the University of Wisconsin-Parkside; University College, Galway; and Delgado Community College, New Orleans. In 1976, he settled into a permanent position at the University of Wisconsin-Milwaukee where he taught Irish Literature, Creative Writing, and Beat Literature until his death in 2008. Loving university life and the stimulation, company and camaraderie that his students' provided, James Liddy eschewed retirement. There was no reason for him to leave a job he enjoyed and American law made it possible for people to work beyond the "traditional retirement age." He continued to be productive with much of his best work being published during the final decade of his life. Though it was his wont to affect a casual air, he was a most productive author.

The American system of teaching literature, as John Montague found out while participating in a seminar taught by American academics in Austria in 1950, was quite different to the system of pedagogy in use in Ireland:

> At times working in the library the atmosphere of American thought drove one frantic: the purely pragmatic approach, the facts and statistics on paper, the theory not an inch beyond reason, technology clamping its artificial structure on creative effort ... The American system of teaching literature was new to nearly all the students, but they approved of it and indications are that it will be adopted in many European universities. They revolted, however, against its product, the diagrams of plots and sub-plots, climaxes and characters, the jargon of the reviews, the competitive newness in poetry (182–83).

However, by the time that James Liddy arrived in San Francisco in 1967 things had changed for the better. New voices had emerged in the academy to challenge the New Critical orthodoxy that so perturbed Montague with the result that the interpretation of literature became more diffuse and complex. Also, the growth of Creative Writing programs brought writers into the universities to teach the many students who sought instruction in writing. One of the main reasons why approaches to reading literary criticism changed in the sixties resulted from the fact that, as Morris Dickstein has pointed out, people had grown "skeptical of the pose of objectivity … It was the artists, with their inherently intense subjectivity, who were quickest to learn that if they expected our credence they had to declare themselves" (248). James Liddy was one such artist and made for his times. As creative writing became more commodified within English departments in the USA, poets and novelists taught literature less and rarely, beyond book reviews, published literary criticism. Liddy, on the other hand, continued to work in various genres – poetry, fiction, criticism – and became a figure able to link the diverse parts of the academic spectrum. Most creative writers in American universities do not see it as part of their job descriptions to write literary criticism while academic critics generally shy away from creative writing. James Liddy, primarily a poet, was adept at all three as well as being an editor and translator. An old-fashioned man-of-letters who had grown-up in a literary culture not dependent on a university, he brought a breadth of experience and expertise to the academy. He would also have agreed, I suspect, with Montague's assertion:

> As for method, I cling to the old-fashioned notion that most of the best criticism is by writers, from Samuel Johnson to John Berryman: they know by training what they are talking about. Writers who are sure of their own gift can often show a warming generosity towards fellow craftsmen … (ix–x).

To suggest that Liddy is a good critic because he is a good poet tells only part of the truth. Of course lessons learned from the practice of writing helped him understand and read literature uniquely; however, Liddy's gifts as a critic are also the result of a lifetime of intense reading and deep thought that add depth, nuance and moral compass to his criticism. The Irish poets of Liddy's generation who have lived or settled in America have written important critical work in addition to the poetry for which they are better known.

When James Liddy arrived in America its universities were lively, forward-looking and well-funded. Though he arrived in San Francisco at an exciting time, when it was at epicenter of liberation and innovation, we should be careful not to overstate the positive. In *Gates of Eden: American Culture in the Sixties*, his backward look at the decade, Morris Dickstein, who began his career as a university professor in 1968, a year after James Liddy had begun his, summarized it as follows:

> There's certainly no reason to take satisfaction in what happened, especially now that the poisonous mood in which the sixties ended has given way to the torpid, constricted climate of the seventies. Though 1968 was one of the nodal years in American history, it's hard to think of one good thing that happened then. The Tet offensive broke the back of our escalation in Vietnam and led to Johnson's withdrawal, but the assassinations of King and Kennedy dashed hopes for nonviolent change, as did the repression in Chicago, the nomination of Humphrey, and the election of Nixon. Within the space of a year the protest movement crested and shattered, and a pernicious right-wing government without principle but with an insidious appetite for power was installed. In retrospect, what followed has all the hallmarks of inevitability. The three chief developments in American public life in the early seventies were not the result of a new phase but merely the garbage of an older one, the unfinished business of the sixties (271).

In the universities, the casual largess of the sixties was replaced by rigidity and conformity operating under the guise of professionalism, as Edmund Wilson has pointed out. Even creative writing was professionalized under the banner of the Associated Writing Programs, an organization that James Liddy disapproved of. Though he was a most productive writer and member of the academy, Liddy preferred to focus on good writing and his students' improvement rather than what he saw as the shallow careerism fostered by the MLA and the AWP. He might walk into a classroom as if he were walking into McDaid's or walk into a bar as if he were arriving at a hall to deliver a lecture. In his body, the ancient and the modern fervently negotiated. About the business of literature, he was serious.

Many of us who live and teach in universities in the American Midwest gather each fall for the annual regional meeting of the American Conference for Irish Studies. Our recent travels have taken us to such cities as Fargo, North Dakota; St. Paul, Minnesota; Chicago, Illinois; Davenport, Iowa; Kansas City, Missouri, to name but a few of the host cities. James Liddy was a regular attendee at these meetings and it was in these settings that many of the earliest versions of his literary essays were first aired. He came to these meetings to engage with the literary and scholarly communities of his adopted region – the American Midwest – and to talk, cajole, gossip and laugh with old friends late into the night. Always an intensely social person and an engaging conversationalist, James Liddy made new friends easily wherever he went. It was always a delight to spend hours in restaurants and bars with him and to hear his opinions on subjects that interested him. His analysis was driven by a curious, original and idiosyncratic mind while his conclusions covered the full range: humorous, inspired, insightful, outrageous, and wildly politically incorrect. He was great company: entertaining, sometimes infuriating, but always lively. Liddy's conversation, intelligence, and his ability to synthesize in original ways the information he had gathered from a lifetime of reading, thought and argument brings to mind similar qualities that Wordsworth identified in Coleridge. Wordsworth likened his friend's conversation to "a majestic river, the sound or sight of whose course you caught at intervals, which was sometimes concealed by forests, sometimes lost in sand, then came flashing out broad and distinct, then again took a turn which your eye could not follow, yet you knew and felt that it was the same river" (Sisman 115). In similar ways, James Liddy's audiences were carried down similar Midwestern rivers on ramshackle rafts. Seated on the edges of rivers (Mississippi, Missouri, Red, Milwaukee), we were energized, entertained and educated by Liddy's remarkable conversational abilities. However, it was often quiet impossible to remember the details the next morning. James Liddy's conversation was but one element of his discourse. It was not as important as what he wrote down and what was published; however, the *blas* present in his conversation made its way into what he wrote. You will learn a great deal from reading these essays and you will also chuckle from time to time at his wit.

For this collection, I have gathered James Liddy's American essays as well as work on figures from the Irish literary Diaspora that he found important such as Joyce and Beckett. Always interested in Spain and having lived there briefly before leaving for the United States, his memoir of traveling there with Michael Hartnett, and his essays on the work of Camilo José Cela and Aidan Higgins, provide further insights into Liddy's sense of the larger literary world. Also included is Liddy's first published essay, "The Figure of Christ in D. H. Lawrence and Edwin Muir" from the *University Review* in 1963, which shows that he might have become a traditional academic literary critic had he wished to take that route. The collection concludes with an interview that Brian Arkins, who has written a monograph on James Liddy's work, conducted with him in *Studies* (1996). As I sought to shape this book, I kept in mind Thom Gunn's *Shelf Life*, the non-fiction of a poet with whom James Liddy had much in common. A second collection, focusing on Irish material, is in preparation and will be published next year.

I am very grateful to the following individuals and institutions that provided support and encouragement for this collection: Alan Hayes of Arlen House invited me to collect and edit these essays and has provided continued enthusiasm for the project. Jim Chapson encouraged me from the outset and provided me with a list of James Liddy's publications and this gift made hunting down copies of the articles and essays a much easier task than anticipated. Though few of the essays were available in digital form, the list that Jim Chapson provided made it possible to access many of them via inter-library loan. Tom Roedel of the Faculty Resource Center at the University of Missouri-St. Louis converted many of the PDFs that I had received via inter-library loan into WORD documents and scanned essays from journals and magazines. Those essays that did not lend themselves to conversion or scanning, I typed myself and I found this task an excellent way of exploring James Liddy's elegant prose style and unique thought progression. Jim Chapson also hunted down hard copies of some essays that I could not locate elsewhere. I am also grateful to Dr. Nora Liddy for her encouragement and for providing materials. The Thomas Jefferson Library at the University of Missouri-St. Louis was also most helpful; in addition to providing me with a warm and inviting place to work, the library's staff was able to locate PDF copies of many of the essays that appear in this volume. Much of the editing of the volume was completed during the wet and cold Irish summer of 2012 and I am grateful to the James Hardiman Library at NUI Galway for providing shelter from the elements and a congenial space to work in. It proved impossible to track down the English language original of one of the essays so I am grateful to Professor Jeanne Morgan Zarucchi of the University of Missouri-St. Louis for translating "Les collines lointaines sont-ellis si vertes? Les vraies images du retour dans la literature irlando-américaine" back into English. To every cow its calf and to every translation its original! I thank my family in the USA and Ireland for their support for this project. Thanks also to the editors of the journals where these essays were originally published. A final thanks to my superiors at the University of Missouri-St. Louis for their support: Dr. Richard Cook, chair of the English Department, and Dr. Joel Glassman, director of the Center for International Studies.

WORKS CITED

Cronin, Anthony. *Dead as Doornails*. Dublin: Lilliput, 1999.

Berryman, John. *The Dream Songs*. New York: Farrar, Straus, and Giroux, 1969.

Dickstein, Morris. *Gates of Eden: American Culture in the Sixties*. New York: Basic Books, 1977.

Montague, John. *The Figure in the Cave and Other Essays*. Antoinette Quinn ed. Syracuse: Syracuse University Press, 1989.

Ryan, John. *Remembering How We Stood: Bohemian Dublin at the Mid Century*. Dublin: Lilliput, 2009.

Sisman, Adam. *Wordsworth and Coleridge: The Friendship*. London: HarperPerennial, 2007.

James Liddy

On American Literature and Diasporas

ONE

A Salute to the Good: My University Life

Then the
worn tracks were smooth &
sharp from use. The cars were
on time & we came & went
as we would,
like perhaps,
adolescent newspapers
gobbled up by
old home towns.

– John Allen Ryan

I went on the plane, the one to London before the one to San Francisco. Michael Hartnett, a very young writer, met me at Heathrow and took me to his house, an hour-long bus ride. I entered the new world flying the polar route on September 11, 1967. That night in San Francisco I made Harrington's at Jones and Market and was asked my particulars of place and race. Next day I saw Robinson Jeffers' house on the beach and threw back my first screwdriver at Nepenthe, a mansion over the Pacific that Orsen Welles had given Rita Hayworth as a wedding present. Later I was to find it as a scene in Kerouac's *Big Sur*.

Next day I made my way to San Francisco State campus, past a nude-in taking place in front of the cafeteria. In the English Department, the assistant gave me a key to BSS 334 and inside the door the man at the other desk introduced himself, "I'm Nic Kubly from New Glarus, Wisconsin." He took me under his wing, after cautioning me that the professor who had my space had just committed suicide. Soon I had an apartment, a condemned basement for sixty-five dollars a month, rented from a bluff Englishman, next to Kubly's place on Waller Street.

My first academic life had started. I was among the flower children who doubled as students. Immediately I was invited to the best parties of my life. Mark Linenthal, the director of the Poetry Center at San Francisco State, acted as magical M.C. In addition to constant dining out at interesting cliquish tables, a gregarious party occurred at Linenthal's on Wednesday afternoons, when the center's reading ended.

My second life with poets began. McDaid's was trumped. Linenthal had me collect James Wright at the airport in a graduate student's car. On our return journey, the poet stopped to order triple gins, a measure I had not before witnessed. Wright loved the Irish, recited Pearse and MacDonagh – we were away! The preceding poet-in-residence John Logan squired me around; we had room service Bloody Marys with Raul Denny in a Union Square hotel. The English chair's party at Sausalito was spectacular: I was introduced to a poet in the program, Stan Rice, married to an Irish girl from New Orleans. Her name was Anne; we discussed Catholic childhoods, both of us born to be priests but fortunately nothing could come of it. Ray West caused a furor at the party by reading a cable from Allan Tate announcing a baby, fertility was honored over the water and craft shops.

My next party was given by the college for new faculty. A famous but sleepy ideologue Dr. Hayakawa came by.

He inquired if I had known his late great friend W.B. Yeats, and then moved on to Beatrice Roethke beside me, informing her he was a friend of her late husband. I recall these occasions as an era of entertaining that would pass in the academy. There was money then, and lots of booze and youngish faculty to consume it. Now puritan harassments and aging baby boomers who have lost their hearts have chilled the departments. One's conversation is at the mercy of the beer-drinking saturnalias of *les jeunes*.

It was endless summer, also the autumn of love – endless glances and glasses. I became intimate with students, as I have been all my working life. Ron Sillman, a poet with a future, started visiting; he was a mailman and told me they held a poetry reading every day in the post office. His father was a cop recruited from the south, by Senator Knowland, to keep Oakland in order. I liked his grandfather's name, Emerald MacMahon. Bill Siverly, an intriguing young literary man who wrote poems about Lorca and José Antonio, knocked on the door in the evenings. I entered into alliance with Jim Chapson when I was invited to be on his master's committee. Fr. Frank McQuilkin was, like Kubly, from Wisconsin, with the same tastes.

Robert Duncan was the eloquent, sarcastic, and long-winded king of all poets. One afternoon at Mark and Francis' he took over: he had just arrived from the march on the Pentagon, where he had glanced into the soldiers' eyes on guard to summon the god of peace. I burst out laughing and he glared. It turned into a two-hour, manic soliloquy. Mark had to murmur when Duncan left, "Robert is heavy today, let us lie on the couches and sleep for an hour."

I met George Stanley and was drawn to the Pacific compound of Jack Spicer whose poetry I began to admire more than any other in the America of his time. Curiously, Linenthal, Schevill, and other San Francisco Staters, could take Duncan but drew the line at Spicer. Robert, in his eccentricities, still played the game. Mark took me to read Spicer's cranky saving-true-poetry letters in the center's files. They rang with absolute integrity. Spicer's circle in Gino's and Carlo's (Aquatic Park in the afternoon) was called by Linenthal "the Hominterm." However, the tide was turning: another former poet-in-residence, Jack Gilbert, graduate students told me, had called them together for an impromptu memorial reading when Spicer died at the age of forty.

My career in America was, in these early years, a mission to meet and salute the good poets. I met them on those Wednesdays. We mobbed each other at the vinous networking: Wright who talked for an hour-and-a-half and then read the poem on the ancient Chinese Governor; Bly, a gaunt Lutheran deacon; Ed Field, who gave the funniest performance and remarked at the party that the conversation of the guests was like eavesdropping on Aldous Huxley's characters asking, "Is it real out there?" Others filled in the slots. Phil Whalen, who I saw was a two-fisted ice-cream eater at the break. Ron Padgett, George Stanley, and Milton Kessler, who suggested I take his place for a semester at Harpur College. John Berryman broke his arm and couldn't come.

An occasion was Greek Independence Day. Cavafy read by Dick Bratset and Thomas Maskaleris. I read after them wearing my blue scarf, given me by Tom Hill, an undergraduate. To my surprise, I was embraced by Duncan and Stanley and by Ruth Witt-Diament, the Center's founder and a friend of Kerouac. Kay Boyle, who had been with James Joyce during a thunderstorm, kissed me, and Linenthal broke in, "Today would have pleased James Joyce, the union of the Irish and the Greek."

I taught two courses a semester, a poetry workshop and the Craft of Poetry, graduate and undergraduate. Some classes I held in Waller Street and supplied the beer. One workshop rotated each week to another student's house. But the tumbrils were arriving at San Francisco State. The fables of professors in assembly couldn't halt them. President Summerskill resigned from an airport payphone. The black student newspaper was raided, the Black Panthers in my class were arrested. The National Guard patrolled the campus surrounded now with barbed wire. William Dickey sank into the bus seat beside me murmuring, "Do you know what my favourite century is? The eighteenth." The administration building was occupied; my heart trembled for my paycheck.

At our back we heard Vietnam marching near. Kay Boyle came to department meetings from Santa Rita prison. We listened to tales of kitchen chores with Joan Baez. Then Governor Reagan got Hayakawa appointed president of San Francisco State and Kay Boyle was fired three times in one day, twice at least through a bullhorn.

The escape from politics, of course, happens through art – my exit door led to the warehouse on Sixth and Mission, where Graham Mackintosh ran the White Rabbit Press. Graham was Spicer's friend and co-maker of his books, and so good that New Directions had tried to hire him. Graham presided over a giant print den where sometimes could be heard the sounds of machines working. The festive days and night culminated in the Natoma Tap Dance Society party, "dedicated to the principles and ideas inherent in the search for truth and beauty thru things on your shoes." I saluted the almost silent presence of Richard Brautigan against a background of Busby Berkeley's movies. The other friend I made was John Allen Ryan, who was having his second book published by the press. John, once bartender at The Place, the holy of holies before Gino's and Carlo's, lived with Robert Berg, State's librarian, who was making plans to defeat the threatened campus strike. Berg, wittiest of that hermetic group!

Jim Chapson survived his Master's diet of Milton, Kafka, and Yeats with Bill Dickey, Ray West, and me. We relaxed and dreamt of a book. And we incorporated an undergraduate friend Tom Hill into it. We designed a San Francisco triptych, led by a Cathay dance, its ringmaster Ezra Pound, with interludes of Cavafy, Zen, Beat, and Catholic masquerades. We took the title Blue House from Tu Fu, "With nothing but the name of drifters in the blue houses."

On the Blue House-warming evening, we entered the great Natoma Cave of Being, so many kinds of beards, costumes, trinkets, we were travelling through Samarkand. The book was not in existence, a thousand hours stretched away, yet one could hear the whir of machines. Who was stoned, who was drunk – only Alan Watts standing there could tell. The machines pounded on, but Graham seemed less interested ... the book began to disappear ... Graham intoned, "Well, I can either go on working on this or I can enjoy the party." The great room exploded into a blizzard of talk, yells, and song-bits. Several laughing hippies carried in placards that proclaimed "San Francisco will enter eternity in the Summer Solstice, 1968."

In September 1969, following Milton Kessler's behest, I arrived at SUNY-Binghamton for the fall semester. After a short sojourn at the chair's house, Mario di Cesare's, Jim and I got billeted at the house of a comparative literature professor, Louis Bolle. My course, besides a poetry workshop, was a *Ulysses* seminar, the one time I have taught Joyce outside Ireland. There was the call to the woods, to woods of anarchy and protest that followed me from San Francisco, but the good women scholars held the class together, staying with the topic. My friends were my colleagues Bernie Rosenthal and Dan Rowe, an inspired instructor – especially on Synge. Larry Keller stood out as a student. He worked in the Gotham Book Mart and a big thrill of his life was recognizing J. D. Salinger. My thrill was being the host of an aged Padraic Colum, the subject of an exhibition organized by Zack Bowen. As he peered into the glass cases in the library, Colum muttered, "They think I'm dead." For me, the bad thrill was Anne Sexton who drank too many Jack Daniels and ate nothing before her reading. I accompanied her on that path. Some dispute evolved between us, in the back seat of the car taking us to the campus reading. I insisted on jumping out and rolled out on the road surface before my house.

My main delight in the Triple Cities was my sub-landlord, Louis Bolle, who had the alacrity of a Frenchman from Geneva. His conversation was Left Bank. He had smuggled currency for Modigliani's mistress, had spoken to Valery in Lyons in the Unoccupied Zone, and, as a student had booed the Geneva Petainist professors wearing their legions of honor on that June day, 1940, when de Gaulle saved France by a broadcast from London. Louis' famous sentences began with the phrase, "I have in mind to ..." and usually contained a request to go somewhere for coffee or a "speedy." He would say to the waitress, "I would like a speedi and make its speedy." When the spedini arrived he would revert the conversation back to dinners with Proust's niece and her husband. He also knew and was encyclopedic about Celeste, Proust's maid. His American epiphany was his first class at Tulane: the belles were in the front rows and so ravishing that he fainted.

In the spring of 1970, I obtained a post of poet-in-residence for a semester at Lewis and Clark College. This was put through by the Dean Anthony Ostroff; I was a replacement for Vern Rutsala. We lived on the campus high over the Columbia River. The beer trail involved the bus that went between Lewis and Clark and downtown Portland. I was intrigued by the division between booze and beer bars and liked particularly the open fish market, but Portland was small after San Francisco. The classes were rich-kid neo-attentive. Jimmy Stewart's daughter was in one of them. The students I got to know best were George Moore and Kevin Wilson.

The essential pleasure of being at Lewis and Clark – apart from Bacchic rites in my cabin under the perpetual wet evergreens – was attending upon Bill Stafford. We met once a week with students in an informal workshop. After Knute Skinner's reading, I blindsided Bill into drinking a second beer, a thing never known before. I recollect his courage after he was appointed to the Library of Congress. On the lawn of the campus, he fielded questions, including hostile ones about his confinement in a pacifist camp during WWII. He had asked me to stand beside him. He liked to talk to me about his days at Berkeley. How he used to sit with his future wife at the back of Jo Miles' class while Spicer and friend, a little tanked, contributed from the front row. I asked what the class was about, and he smiled, "Yeats."

My stint at Denison University was longer and more severe. This distinguished college was set in bucolic leafage. It was town for retired ministers; the two inns were still in prohibition. Just before I arrived, the administration had taken out of its teachers' contract a prohibition against having alcohol in one's house. I did not survive very well. We had to travel for beer by the odd bus to Newark, the seat of Licking County, where there was a definite Klan whiff. The classes were relaxed, but when the students were good, they were very good. I encouraged them to bring their guitars to class to break up my Utopian monotony. My colleagues were kind. The chair, Ken Marshall, a gentleman. Paul Bennett and Tony Stoneburner engaging radicals. The latter drove me to Kenyon to see John Crowe Ransom, who met us at the door with a tall Scotch in hand. He was engaged in the mutilation of his early classical poems for a new edition; Tony gave him words of caution. It was delightful evening in another century. Ransom informed us he had heard that Lowell was behaving in a very "rusty" fashion.

I lived in the College Town House, in an old apartment on the main street next to Sally Jones' hotel. Soon I was presiding over an exhaustive social crossroads. Writers passed through, but not in the rapturous manner of San Francisco State. I gave a party for Adrienne Rich after her reading. We debated women and the church: I recited the long roll of women saints; she was half-convinced perhaps. She had difficulty in going down our long stairs, so a burly student took her up in his arms and carried her down. I had a somber afternoon with Tony Hecht in which future threats to the canon were foreseen and given proper curses; we adjoined to the hotel next door, where Hecht had a bottle in his room. The climax of the not wholly happy year in Granville was the visit of Katherine Kavanagh in our last week there. This became the last time the College Town House was under beer siege: students swept around Katherine in inchoate sympathy. The proceedings initiated with a reading of the 1916 Proclamation. Katherine was on an American tour, a pilgrimage that took us, together with my most brilliant student Hank Schlau, to the crazy lounges of Thames Street, Newport, Rhode Island – a fight breaking out every five minutes. Finally Katherine and I rested in a room in the Chelsea Hotel in New York. As I left Denison, I noticed someone had changed the gate motto from "Know you the truth and the Truth shall make you free" to "the Truth shall make you Freak."

Thence I came not to Carthage but to Parkside; Lord, thou pluckest me out in the Midwest. Tucked in to the Kenosha side of the county line, a new campus was arising from fresh fields and woods, a pastoral landscape for students now bearing the narcissistic – not the political – part of the 1960s. They smoked pot and consumed beer as if there was not to be a conservative tomorrow. They exalted the moment, the nonthinking college moment, and went off to party. Kubly had arranged my job. He was a friend of the chancellor, a labor scholar. Andy McLean, a Scottish Shakespearean, as many of them have been, put us up in his house until we got an apartment in Parkside Village. There we were joined by Will Reisner, from Honolulu, a neophyte in liberation pastoral. I spent some weekends at Kubly's New Glarus farm, sipping in the William Tell setting. This Wisconsin Swiss town put on its annual apple-off-the-head show on Kubly's farm. My courses were involved with Irish cultural as well as literary studies. The main event of the second semester was the St. Patrick's Day festival with Knute Skinner, William Cotter Murray, and a symposium on John Ford's movie *The Informer,* with the wicked and dynamic acting of MacLiammóir in the title role. Irish scholars Janet and Gareth Dunleavy gave papers. This was the beginning of an affinity with them that led to my progress up the lakeshore to the University of Wisconsin-Milwaukee in 1976.

The intervening period was taken up with a year's teaching at University College, Galway, under my friend Lorna Reynolds, followed by a year of blissful Bohemian excess in New Orleans. I lived in the French Quarter, two blocks from Bourbon Street, and I took the trouble, as they say, to jump into the Cajun, Creole, and Latin life of that river town. The bars did not close their doors. The bartenders, as I was Irish, bestowed free drinks. I taught four courses at Delgado Community College, near the museum and Degas' house, for a paltry sum. My only time teaching composition – but that didn't spoil the fun! I didn't mix with a single great writer for a year and that was a kind of serenity. But New Orleans is a different story from my academic forays, and I will tell it in another place.

So back to Wisconsin, this time to Milwaukee, a calm metropolis of leafy trees on broad avenues and parks and

German socialism in the ancient parts of its system, with the long lake nesting against the campus. Janet and Gareth were more than welcomers. They had an apartment for me when I arrived. Their affection for me was constant and I was happy to build up an Irish Studies program with Mel Friedman and them. I also worked in the company of writers like Tom Bontly, Jim Hazard, and John Goulet, of whom I am indeed fond and obligated to. I have been, for more than twenty-five years, a Tuesday and Thursday man, with lunch added, with a committee seat in the Creative Writing Program. I have had a number of Ph.D. writers under my wing. To number some: Bob Brown, Joe Gahagan, Cynthia Belmont, Bryan Tomasovich, Jayson Iwen, Tyler Farrell, Eric Adams, Erich Ebert. Among undergraduates have been undeniable promisers and achievers, to name a few: Tim Anderson, Robert Thompson, Matt Cook, Diane Unterweger, Lauren McCool, Keith Gaustad, last but not least Zack Pieper.

Many writers have passed through Milwaukee. For me, the most interesting visitor has been John Ashbery. I had long bewitchment with him in the restaurant across from Curtin Hall. When someone asked him to autograph his art piece in *Newsweek,* he poured his Bombay gin over it. A presence was Robert Stone who, at the same time every day, 4pm, in the same restaurant, asked a similar question, "What is the difference between Fianna Fáil and Fine Gael?" Bill Stafford sat on my couch and we talked the subtle diplomacy of poets. He was still a saint. Allen Ginsberg gave two vast rallies of his extraordinary public poetry, but Charles Bukowski was blasted, or pretended to be, at a slightly smaller convocation. Ginsberg wanted a brewery tour, and Bukowski said, in Axel's, "I will only talk to sons of mailmen." We were happy to provide him with one. Finally, he and sons of mailmen woke up at 3am, the professor holding the check for the reading with shouts of "Deliver the Goods." Professor Harrold had been nervous about handing it over for fear of the drink. Robert Duncan came to a party in my Locust Street place, rang Jess Collins, and made off with a student, all in a matter of minutes. My favorite reading of these years was Helen Adam's in Woodland Pattern. She sang, danced, lunged, wanded her ballades and ghost words with supernatural strength. She was a goddess, a witch, a diva. She had come over with her mother and sister in 1939 from Scotland for a wedding and they had been unable to return during the war. Never was writing so regional, but what region? Adam had been part of the San Francisco Renaissance, and I talked to her about Jack Spicer, "He was a gentleman and a fine poet. I regretted his death."

I am certain of a few things. One should know one's students and one should tell them at least who the good poets of the last half century are. There are a few good poets and a few good students. We are blessed. I teach Irish literature, Beat literature, and poetry workshops. The instructor must dance, nay, tiptoe the line between enjoying his job and a hesitant approach to responsibility. There is a duty to legend higher than to college administration.

An Sionnach (2005)

A Problem with Sparrows: Spicer's Last Stance

I arrived in San Francisco too late to see Jack Spicer but I arrived in San Francisco to meet him. There are only a few poets in a poet's life and you must be on time (a good poet's life is a series of triumphs). Spicer though invisible was still around in 1967, out in the fog amongst the quick and the singing. I was introduced to his invisibility by three friends, Graham Mackintosh, John Allen Ryan, and Robert Berg. George Stanley took me over the ground more than once, "The ground still squirming. The ground still not fixed as I thought it would be ..." The "false ground" of a country he left, not without reluctance and with ten books.

Graham confirmed my acquired lore from Dublin: what poets talk about who have made it are their accountants and when they haven't it's chairmen and editors, "Jack at a party said what he wanted to say, and one cannot succeed that way." The early sense of what I wanted to hear from Spicer: that he was accused of being more interested in truth than in poetry. He was obviously a person in a hurry with messages – something godlike had happened. Younger, I yearned for such an Orphic voice formulating out of nowhere, the animal-remembering power, as barbarously yawping as the discoverer of the country Spicer had to leave, Whitman. His critics at San Francisco State who warned me against Spicer's North Beach hominterm bleated like Thoreau when confronted with the Calamus poems, "He does not celebrate love at all. It is as if the beast spoke." Yet Spicer was more delicate with less of a Victorian constitution, both as Ariel and Caliban (obviously Spicer was both), than the poet who heard the America he had invented singing. Spicer could not fulfill Whitman's self image-dream, "Merlin strong and wise and beautiful at 100 years old." Even if the dream was positioned not towards wisdom but magic; magic that without God comes too close to wisdom. "Rimbaud without wings."

Of his last book, posthumously published, it's not enough to agree with Blaser in "The Practice of Outside" (his commentary included in *The Collected Books of Jack Spicer)* that the writing is surreal or under the real. It is simply a message, stark and reductively absolute as, the life lived the craft eclipsed, last statements or testaments are wont – a message, if it comes from anywhere, of ghost-voices from under the world. In all that fable of dictation theory that Spicer so elaborately goldleafed from Wordsworth and Yeats, the breathing of this already ghosting man (1964–65) into minimal staccato poetry! *Book of Magazine Verse* as gasps, as funeral sighs, substituting for rites (the repeated poem in the book beginning "Pieces of the past arising out of the rubble" must be reheard, for it is a rubric for a solemn dirge: vain rest, vain words for it), serves as the context for the death of the poet, the passing of King Cock, as it were on a dung hill, among the shadows of the future and the peculiar shapes of the past. And yet it says, Poetry is impersonal, one is not present as hero or victim even in death.

Book of Magazine Verse is divided into "books" with names of magazines that reflect a national or a Californian establishment. Some, if not most, are literary; others are radical-Catholic like *Ramparts,* and *The St. Louis Sporting News* is here for the irresistible baseball reference and the idea of "fixing." The poetics as poems thrust against the managers of each industry (including the poetry industry), the "Captains." *Poetry Chicago* and *The Nation* are corrupt corporations threatening both good poetry and promising young poetry. It is proper to ask why Robin Blaser, in editing *The Collected Books,* left out the dedication to *Book of Magazine Verse,* a mock acknowledgement of the rejection of the poems by editors Levertov and Rago. This seems as vital to me as the original cover – *The Collected Books* should at the very least have had the covers of each volume as illustrations – a take-off of the Pegasus drawing of *Poetry Chicago,* Spicer was a symbolist brother of Oscar Wilde, who said of his books, "I always begin with the cover." The merging of cover, paper, and poems was possible only with small non-commercial presses: a point Spicer must have wanted to make. The varying colors of each part in the first edition makes us remember Dorian Gray choosing different colors for his ten large paper editions of Á *Rebours:* one to suit each mood. The paper of *Book of Magazine Verse* imitates the paper of the original publications. Newsprint for *The St. Louis Sporting News* and glossy paper for *Downbeat,* a jazz magazine. Aesthetic considerations mostly moved Spicer; the protest against selling out was, like the fluttering butterfly modes of Wilde and Firbank, an urge to preserve beauty in decay against the coming mass-produced apocalypse of coffee table books and paperbacks.

The manifesto of 35 poems (with one repeat) pushes towards extremes, past the author and beyond his targets but straight as an arrow towards the source of poetry, not just the "outside," where he knew it could no longer be a community but at least a flame. His bullshit quota full, a warrior for authenticity (real lives make good poems), Spicer had a virile, almost militaristic rage. His career seems a parade of warnings, this the final admonition: "No/ One accepts this system better than poets. Their hurts healed for a few dollars." "These big trucks drive and in each one/ There is a captain of poetry or a captain of love or a captain of sex." "The road-captains, heartless and fast-moving ..." Simultaneous with the composition of these dire charges we have the tape of the Berkeley Poetry Festival talk and answer a month before his death. Here Olson is named as a big captain, the market is analyzed for the young poet who wants to go there to sell out, and specifically *Poetry* is mentioned. We are told we cannot or shouldn't appear there because of whom our poems will have to rub shoulders with; when we are published in a magazine we become part of that community. It is as simple as being told to mind who our friends are – and, seeing the ersatz and low mimetic culture of published poetry now, we should take Spicer seriously. I do.

The first level theme then is the attack on the venality of being published in terms of politics not poetry. *Poetry* is what *U.S. News & World Report* would be to a devout Trotskyist. The spawning assaults, spurts of coherence fanning out to isolated statements of an absolute ideology, transvaluate the original privacy of the ideas. They also suggest exhaustion of his working methods.

We have assembled here, in ascending degree of traditionalism, in addition to the poet who protests the system and the bosses, two other central fortress positions: 1) the classic love poet in dying heat, and 2) the Christian believer a witness to transcendence and beguiled, as a preliminary, in "sweet Platonic spiritland." The main love poems are in the *Tish* and *Downbeat* sections. For the while I will just look at *Tish,* 2, where climate interacts with a love situation. The lover shivers at ten above freezing, becomes a bird flying through snow-clouds, nestles in the poet's palm. The lover becomes an Arctic snow goose "if there are such things" and finally a sparrow about to starve in snow, 30 below in the hand-holding of lover and poet. "A problem with sparrows." Spicer is wonderfully in the Roman tradition, the other is a *puer delicatus* of a male lover (add to this the folk belief of the lecherous nature of the birds, "The adulterous sparrows in the eaves"). As we are meant to, we go to the second "Lesbia" poem of Catullus, where his girl's sparrow is dead that "quern plus illa oculis Buis amabat." The image of Lesbia caressing her bird in her hand is presented as her way of dampening down the flames of passion – a clear explanation in part of what is wrong in the *Tish* poem. Catullus and his world do not seem alien to Spicer, as they have not to other writer-lovers. For the designated heroes and victims (the poets of love), being in love constitutes a way of life, as Kenneth Quinn makes plain in his *The Catullan Revolution*. Love is a serious preoccupation for this kind of imagination, the *Praeceptor Amoris*. It is usual and traditional to engage in the pursuit of love with a young man; it is also usual and traditional that one's affairs stay at a frequent and casual level. It is this latter proposition that Spicer animadverts against. Passion is not quite sincerity, and what we have is the Christian reality (about the person) psychotically disturbing "the offered good." But when it is not offered, as in *Tish*, 3, conscience, having found a soul, is a consolation. But we know consolation is not for love. Belief without morals is what we Christian poets spread as merchandise. A problem with doves.

The final meaning of *Book of Magazine Verse* is that of a man at the end of his tether having to find a way out, and finding it in the Incarnation, the flesh on the poem of God. It is the melody of Job, past patience yet redemptive. There is no dark brewing lament like it. It is Osip Mandelstam's, "I drink the cold mountain air of Christianity." Mandelstam is a Christian poet of ultimates, one aware of Dante's rose in Paradise and Villon's "lyrical hermaphroditism." If only Spicer had been drinking on Russian Hill with Mandelstam, instead of the Celtic bore, Dylan Thomas, with no idea of history's cornucopia!

Mandelstam's inspired essay on Villon contains a sentence which seems to sum up Jack's psychic nature: "By his very nature, a lyric poet is a bisexual creature, capable of an infinite number of fissions in the name of his inner dialogue." Since Jesus is celibate, both man and woman on the cross, the poetry in this book is affirmative atonement material, with genitals appearing only to have access to the body. The soul is a sweet place, untouched yet untouchable. Ambiguities of vinegar and spear. Christsperm of "no love deserves the death it has."

The remainder of this paper will be simply a sequence of notes on individual poems. The poems for *The Nation* have been assimilated. So I start with the *Poetry* magazine satirica. Poems are section-numbered.

1 The good of the heterosexual bourgeois world is easily maintained. The world of the homosexual/artist (because Spicer equates them here) is beautiful and magical but useless in the social sense. As in Auden's Yeats, "Poetry makes nothing happen." With a subtheme: the fading poems of past ("sickened by the old lemon") issues of *Poetry*.

2 The repeat, the rebaked poem, in the Hamlet metaphor, for those unfamiliar with funerals.

3 The first part of the poem posits the nothingness of matter (the luxuriant jungle and drunken conversation). The other part is the bar/war dream of being back with mother.

4 In saying the rind is also called the skin, Spicer declares that he is talking about human fruits. Oranges remain oranges in the world of marriage and regeneration, as symbolized by the circular shape of the orange. Lemons

are oval – not a continuing line. The love and life of the artist/homosexual, though more fully continuous, is not self-perpetuating. It comes to an end and stops, like love stops.

5 Aging and time – though one learns to better read the symbols one forgets the essential (ideal?) love (good?) which these symbols manifest. A position which includes the possibility that disregards the obviously half-correct Freudian interpretation because that interpretation forgets the informing original love.

6 Physical love seems awkward, material, the skins are material objects such as the bedclothes, and frustrating. But it gives rise to the "good dream" of spiritual (ghostly) love, "the ghost of myself and the ghost of yourself … With/ Out/ Skin." "The moment's rest" as distinct from "a moment's rest" (orgasm).

Tish

1 Again the Platonic of the real and ideal – here with real "rubble" of the mind. This essence, its capacity for art and love, astonishes. The image of dancing is continued from the last poem. Of course it was to Cocteau, not Nijinsky, that Diaghilev said, "Etonez moi." "A crazy notion in a grey society." A notion commemorative of all the artist-lovers of the Ballet and Paris at its apogee is contrasted with American present, California's imitations. It was Nijinsky who, through his unacceptable relationship (a kind of erotic tutoring) with Diaghilev, rejuvenated choric theatre with the triumphs of the Ballet Russe. The beauty of Nijinsky or the beauty of any youth able to dance (and dancing) comes from a long distance and takes getting used to. It is "The whorship of beauty/ Or beautiful things take a long time getting used to" (ninth poem in the "Thing Language"

section of *Language*). "What you hear is what you have heard from," similar to Plato's "All knowledge is memory." The last line is a (Christian?) reminder of mortality.

2 Lesbia's sparrow. Already dealt with except for this late reflection: the problem of trying to love someone who is so starved for love that they cannot return it.

3 We refuse, the horse-animal inside us refuses, love (Grace) while pretending to ourselves that it is being refused for us, As Odysseus pretended he wanted to return to wife and son. Love is as great as it should be – if we properly know how to drive Plato's black and white horses of *The Phaedrus.* Refusing to drink the water imagining, neurotic Narcissi, that the water refuses us. Though the heroic(?) Greek Age is over, despite temporary returns like the Renaissance, human nature is not altered. We are parasites because we won't allow love to work.

Ramparts

1 Plato (mouth) is not Christ (heart). Salvation exists. The Piltdown Man, beloved of Teilhard de Chardin, was a forgery. Evolution cannot be hurried, or the gaps that discoverable. On the other hand, Plato's fire is real flame: the shadows of love are the shadows of God. Balloons make an attempt at transcendence but the real lack of it ("the sky where men weep for men") leads to the sterility of the moon and the artificial distances of space travel. However, it is not that distant, the individual soul can reach it; Beatrice guides Dante to light.

2 The apparent contradictions of divine truth, the strangeness of Rome as the holy city. St. Peter, the rock, denying – Jesus divine becoming human – the church human accepting divinity. These *are,* and cannot be denied any more than, and are as persuasive as, "the weather." Despite Pius XII's hiccups, or Peter in the courtyard, it's a "rock" – the old pun for turning Augustus' empire from marble to church stone. Spicer's ideas are close to the Roman poems of Osip Mandelstam. "It's not Rome, as a city, that lasts forever,/ but man's place in the universe ... without it houses, and altars,/ are contemptible rubble, pitiful, wretched." Or from his slightly later poem on Benedict XV's Peace Encyclical, "There is a spirit/ risen and leavened by freedom,/ fate of the sweetest. The Roman priest survives/ centurion-eyes catching absolutely the music." Mandelstam's Romanism came from his nostalgia for a world culture, the unity of the medieval world.

3 The perishing of the good leaders, Pope John, JFK. A little Protestant reaction here like Mandelstam's Orthodox guilty retractions. Spicer would probably prefer different Papal costumes and would avoid travel to Texas.

4 The technological world could not exist without God. This is Spicer's big statement: the apparently gratuitous gift of Grace creates humanity. Job-Spicer wonders why God bothers, why He is not a misanthrope. These poems show an essentially humanist distaste for all gnosis.

The St. Louis Sporting News

1,2,3,4. These poems are about playing by (obeying) the rules (divine laws and laws of poetry) or not. The rules are difficult, sometimes impossible to follow or understand – but any attempt to cheat them is both a sell-out and self-destructive (i.e., in contrast, perhaps, being destroyed by the rules?). 1 and 2 are about selling out, 3 and 4 are about not selling out. 4 returns to the concerns of the *Ramparts* poems: the necessity of having to accept God despite his false images.

Vancouver Festival

1 Building Augustine's city of God in the wilderness. The city is an extension of a baseball diamond (baseball is still symbolic of the divine laws). The diamond is a metaphor of perfection; therefore building a city outward and from the baseball diamond is building an eternal, beautiful city. Reminiscent of Hopkins' "This Jack, joke, poor potsherd, patch, matchwood, immortal diamond is immortal diamond."

2 Los Angeles is a parody of the city of God. Though it has lost Faith and Charity streets it still has Hope Street. This makes the quest possible despite "the idiocy of age and direction" as the poet goes north to find the source of the (mortal) chill in his bones.

3 Thingness, home (lambs – lamb of God) surviving in the world of matter. Last sun falling, direction ending.

4 Still it doesn't cohere (Pound on *The Cantos).* The landscape a "mess of nature" without supernatural qualities. Pioneers' errors.

5 The Beatles, equated in the Ferlinghetti letter with trendiness, the paperback culture that renders middle-class values immovable and horrifying, make Spicer think of exit and escape. There is no point in living with the Beatles playing on the records (or on the jukebox in North Beach). The impossible (a right exit) is possible but not, obviously, obvious.

6 The important thing is the individual moment of truth, courageous action, not the apparent goal: "Dead bait." Even if your truth is small.

7 Detachment – disinterested love. The immigrants turned back on themselves, the San Francisco poets back after this temporary migration to Vancouver. Even the Prime Minister's face is "parched."

Downbeat (placed last for its name an ironic tribute to Kerouac?)

1 The bad East – Olson wanting everyone to believe in the ships in "Gloucester Harbor." The West, the coast, with its dead-end possibilities, "nothing but ocean," grabbing "the first thing coming." No comfort.

2 Thingness again. Confronting the world without dreams or illusions. Desert.

3 The self is "light baggage." Lacking substance, important only as direction which begins to mock itself, reminiscence in distraction.

4 Beware of the established bosses or "makers." Their music is lies. If you find the true music, outside of them, you will be young, still beautiful. Advice to a Canadian: keep British Columbia young and as free as possible from Capitalism, its chance is its out-of-the-way position?

5 Poets are ludicrously easy to buy. The ridiculous selling-out price of the poets. Fame, respect. The absurdity of the ordinary imagination, what the poets get into.

6 Portrait of the real poet as aspiring angel (desert butterfly).

7 The Pacific roaring with love though "Its beaches we've starved on." New tide, new surf, creation. "A spirit moved upon the waters."

8 The passing anonymity of people. Incorrectly or loosely called guerillas, nameless as Trotsky was a name. Names for the nameless; unknown Christians, for instance, with that name.

9 Charity. Love at last, the last glimpse. Possible to hold hands together – the poet doesn't lie if he can do this.

10 The shit of the world, Ginsberg the false poet pretending the young are not part of it, that it is not there. Ginsberg's abstract impersonal "love" which is not even love really, only a "name" – a gesture, a rhetoric. False prophet for America emotionally dying. Spicer concludes with a hint of successful prosecution. The point of his whole enterprise is that people die because they cannot make the right moral judgments.

Postscript. As it becomes increasingly clear that Spicer is a unique poet differing from the others in the San Francisco Renaissance, because of his honesty and objective power to distinguish the true from false in literature (and after his death whipping the big names out of the Californian temple of the imagination), his cult will become vast and sulfurous like a religion. The poet turns into a shrine. One hears and feels the rapture of the pilgrims already, one thinks of all the poems offered to him. My favorite is Harold Dull's elegy for him in *The Star Year.* Dull enters the hillside, whose expanse shimmers with the orange wings of dead monarchs: a superimposition of childhood, chasing butterflies, and his last winter with Jack on the hillside presence. The new butterflies are "ghosts" reflecting visibility and invisibility. Candleflames or water. It is the wind which vibrates the wings of dead monarchs, back to the mobility of the "squirming" ground.

boundary 2 (1977)

WORKS CITED

Quinn, Kenneth. *The Catullan Revolution*. Ann Arbor, Michigan. University of Michigan Press, 1971.

Spicer, Jack. *Book of Magazine Verse*. Stan Persky ed. San Francisco; White Rabbit Press, 1966.

... The *Collected Books of Jack Spicer*. Robin Blaser ed. San Francisco: Black Sparrow Press, 1975.

WITH THE KINGS:
JACK KEROUAC'S *ON THE ROAD* AT 50

The anniversaries are piling up quickly for the Beat writers of the 1950s and 1960s whose work created vital new distinctions in aesthetics and culture. The middle part of the 1950s was the nexus for the best and most dynamic publishing of the writers who came out of the blue in post-second World War America. They challenged the conformity heralded by the shift to the suburbs and the Cold War right-wing surge personified by the rise of Senator Joseph McCarthy.

In particular, the novelist Jack Kerouac and the poet Allen Ginsberg, comrades in arms, came on the world stage to reacquaint readers with the old holiness of the imagination signaled here by free expression and spontaneity. The impact of their first major work filled a vacuum caused by a change in cultural norms that was the result of the Second World War. The emergence of Kerouac and Ginsberg as potential world magicians triggered an urge for experiment and defiance that marked two decades.

Ginsberg's reading of *Howl* at the famous Gallery 6 in San Francisco is commonly accepted as inaugurating the Beat movement on October 7th, 1955. It was shortly afterwards brought out by Ferlinghetti's City Lights imprint. Kerouac's *On the Road* was published by Viking 50 years ago today, with a blurb by its editor Malcolm

Cowley invoking Hemingway and the Lost Generation. The Lost Generation always had an autumnal feeling; the Beats feel like spring excess.

More than the 1920s writers or other Beats, Kerouac had "writing soul". His advice "burn, burn, burn, like fabulous yellow Roman candles exploding like spiders across the stars" described his characters capering on the American highways.

Kerouac had little idea his words would be epochal, that he would reconfigure the American landscape in literature. He captured the warmth of people who lived and worked that landscape in molten, flamboyant language in a manner that had not been done before. Gilbert Millstein's strongly favourable review in the *New York Times* was published on the same day the book appeared. Within a month, *On the Road* was on the best-seller list. It is not surprising that all his books are in print. Viking will publish an anniversary edition of *On the Road* this year, and will also be publishing in book form the original scroll version of the work. The Library of America will include it in a collection of Kerouac's "road novels". The book captured the world; its rhythms were universal in their reach.

Marlon Brando wanted to make a film about Neal Cassady, the central figure of the novel; Warner Brothers made an offer for it. The book roared through all sections of society, despite some negative reviews, was praised by many in the art communities and taken up by Bob Dylan, Janis Joplin, Van Morrison, David Amram, David Bowie and Jim Morrison.

Kerouac has been a crucial reference in music by singers such as Tom Waits and Willie Nelson and bands such as 10,000 Maniacs, the Beastie Boys and Morphine.

The effect took some time to reach Ireland, but to take two examples, Patrick Kavanagh said in 1965 in Evanston, Illinois: "in fact I would say the only people in America that are alive are men like Jack Kerouac. *On the Road* is an excellent book, one of my favourite books about America." And in his poem, "To Jack Kerouac", Cathal Ó Searcaigh apostrophized the author, "I didn't see Min a'Leagha or Fana Bhuí then, but the plains of Nebraska and the grassy fields of Iowa/and when the blues came it wasn't the Bealtaine Road that beckoned but a highway crossing America" (translation by Sara Berkeley).

In the current issue of the *Nation*, Jonah Raskin notes both the 50th anniversary of *On the Road* and the centennial of Jack London's *The Road*. London's volume describes the down-and-outs of America's industrial age, a sort of romantic but realistic Orwellian narrative. Kerouac's opus takes a path through a continent where many incomes are rising to middle-class levels and the media controls a mass market. Like London, Kerouac became disillusioned, but his reaction was a spiritual one; he expounded on the "Beatitude" root of the word "Beat" and advocated dropping out of society and its materialisms.

Mike Wallace asked Kerouac on TV: "This Beat Generation is a 'seeking generation' ... what are you looking for?" The response: "God. I want God to show his face." Kerouac viewed writing not as a profession but as an act of faith in a confession where he would be both the joyful and the melancholy penitent. Increasingly, he turned more obviously to religion, to both his original Catholicism and Buddhism. Ginsberg wrote: "As Jack grew older, in despair and lacking the means to calm his mind and let go of the suffering, he tended more and more to grasp at the Cross ... seeing himself on the Cross and finally conceiving of himself as crucified." His identity, however, was always flexible, "He could be a sophisticated litterateur or an old drunk alternatively."

Kerouac was proud of *On the Road* but he preferred *Visions of Cody* or *Doctor Sax*. Personally, I like the middle-to-late period of *Tristessa, Visions of Gerard* and *Big Sur* where the form is shorter and more integrated with images and poetic language. *On the Road* achieved primary myth; it gave a new description of the mobile, state-savvy, going west, male-bonding, American hero who is also an American goof in the person of Dean Moriarty (Neal Cassady). It is an inclusive book, extending the range of American autobiography in perceptive ways to west coast city inhabitants, Bohemians, working-class people and Mexicans.

Kerouac's hotly composed scenes of modern jazz in San Francisco are superb, "Holy flowers floating in the air were all these tired faces in the dawn of Jazz America." Note those holy flowers! The book is intended as a gospel. Ihab Hassan has written on the Beat novel: "Its gospel is a gospel of wonder and love." Kerouac's penchant for self-revelation, increasingly relevant to his career, focused on religious consciousness. This return to God-language was paradoxically accompanied by a reawakening of the possibilities of Dionysian revelry.

The latter was part of the Beat canon, a gift to society described by Leslie Fiedler as "the last, mad efflorescence of the dreams of utopian sex." Spin-offs from the Kerouac legend continue. Examples include a Beat Week at Barnes & Noble in Minneapolis: Monday, a Naked Lunch special; Tuesday, Spontaneous Prose (readings from Beat authors); Wednesday, Live Performance (jazz); Thursday, Coffee House Open Poetry; Friday, Brave New Workshop Performance (dramatic riffs on Beat writers).

Beat courses are now more common on campuses. Hofstra University offered a course in 1992: *An American Odyssey: Art and Culture Across America*, costing $3,450 in tuition; 29 Beat cities for six credits. The bus driver dressed like Buffalo Bill and was "something of a 1990s refugee from the 1960s world of *Easy Rider*".

In 2004 the first draft of *On the Road*, written on a scroll that rolls over 120 feet of paper smudged with editing marks, began a 13-stop, four-year national tour of museums and libraries. It had been bought by Indianapolis Colts owner Jim Irsay for $2.43 million, the largest price ever paid for a literary manuscript. When it arrived at Marquette University in Milwaukee, local poets (including this writer) welcomed it with readings in the campus stone cold chapel of Joan of Arc. Before this event, for a number of years in Milwaukee, the novel was read from start to finish in a tavern on Jack's birthday.

There exist a number of interesting connections between Kerouac and Ireland (I am indebted to the poet Michael Begnal for his research). In *Vanity of Duluoz,* a late novel, Kerouac recalls his glimpse of Ireland from a Merchant Marine ship during the second World War: "I stood there crying, my eyes pouring tears, I said to myself 'Ireland? Can it be? James Joyce's country?'"

In a letter in 1952 to Allen Ginsberg, Kerouac wrote of *On the Road,* "it is like Ulysses and should be treated with the same gravity." There has been, of late, critical speculation that the Celtic oral tradition was involved in in Kerouac's story-telling skills and strongly efficient memory.

Kerouac was impressed and a little influenced by *Finnegans Wake*. In *Big Sur,* one of the most probing and devastating accounts of alcoholism ever published, the protagonist listens to and attempts to decipher the sounds of the sea – Joyce's last project idea. The novel *Maggie Cassidy* gives an account of a high-school affair with an Irish-American girl that invokes lyric images of Ireland but, typically for an American of that period, they are also sentimental: "The dark flowing enriched heart – Irish as peat, dark as Kilkenny night, sorcerous as elf, red-lipped as red-rubied morn on the Irish sea on the east coast … bringing tears to my eyes to be an Irishman too and lost and sunk inside her for ever …"

Kerouac could specially envision the heart of the US because his imagination was seized there by impulses he explored. However, one should also recall his devotion to and evocation of Mexico in *On the Road* and *Tristessa*. His writing about that country was always poignant and beautiful. William Burroughs, the most articulate member of the Generation, says it best: "Kerouac was a writer. That is, he wrote."

The Irish Times (2007)

THE ARCHITECTS OF THE VICTORY OF LOVE: PATRICK KAVANAGH AND THE BEAT GENERATION

On a cold day in Evanston, Illinois, in 1965, Patrick Kavanagh stood in the American academic temple and uttered certain ideas and phrases that seemed blasphemous to many. His prophetic pose on the occasion of a symposium on poetry after Yeats reflected a typical stance: that the artist appears in society from under the boughs of the tree of life. He spoke of his American compatriots on the same journey as himself. This was an arms-across-the-Atlantic moment, and the casting out of the respected in favour of those who should be revered:

> In fact I would say the only people in America that are alive are men like Jack Kerouac. *On the Road* is an excellent book, one of my favourite books about America since Henry Miller's *The Air-Conditioned Nightmare,* and I like Corso, Ferlinghetti, and Allen Ginsberg very much. (*Triquarterly* 4, 1965)

Special generations on earth seem to be the providence of God, and if a member of one is not chairperson of any board, there still seems to be some law of cyclical return. I first noticed this in relation to Yeats's "Irish Literary Renaissance". I remember the full blast of this idea when I began reading Yeats's prose. In his essay, "The Autumn of the Body", the conditions for "new" returns are predicted out of never-ending weariness: "Man has wooed and won the world, and has fallen weary, and not, I think, for a time, but with a weariness that will not end until the last autumn, when the stars shall be blown away like withered leaves."

Note the siren of the apocalypse, now the siren of the holocaust and the atomic blast, which the Beat Generation saw and heard and reacted to in the 1950s. In the underground, "alternative" culture of the North American coasts, it was, so to speak, always autumn and never summer – the mainstream family had faded like the Fourth of July. Now it was time for experiments with literary form, poetics, ideas, performance, jazz, as well as with libido in general. No wonder, after sportive visits to the grand old bookshop in Dublin, Hodges Figgis in Dawson Street, to buy another set of City Lights books that were changing my world, I began to see the situation in terms of the *fin de siécle.* I began in my own psyche as a new poet to adjust and embody this:

> Come, heart, where hill is heaped upon hill:
> For there the mystical brotherhood
> Of sun and moon and hollow and wood
> And river and stream work out their will;
>
> And God stands winding His lonely horn,
> And time and the world are ever in flight;
> And love is less kind than the grey twilight
>
> And hope is less dear than the dew of the morn.
>
> – "Into the Twilight"

reads as Yeats's 1895 invocation to Allen Ginsberg's *Howl,* Jack Kerouac's *Dharma Bums,* and William Burroughs *Naked Lunch.* Yeats's earlier rose and berry eating attitudes set the mood for decadence, both individually and esoterically, and proceeded naturally to calculate and catalogue its effects. The horn of Yeats's God is perhaps lonely because it is empty, whereas for the most part the Beat horn is the source of jocundity and comradeship.

Again, Yeats's ethereal effervescence is outmanoeuvred by American concepts of blood, muscle, and sinew. Cultural differences remain, but the curtain rises on the same *mise-en-scéne.*

I would like to show how "Beat" Yeats was, and to suggest that 1895 and 1955 were mutual releases and stirrings. My quotation comes from Yeats's essay, "Discoveries":

> I took the Indian hemp with certain followers of Saint-Martin on the ground floor of a house in the Latin Quarter. I had never taken it before, and was instructed by a boisterous young poet, whose English was no better than my French. He gave me a little pellet, if I am not forgetting, an hour before dinner, and another after we had dined together at some restaurant. As we were going through the streets to the meeting place of the Martinistes, I felt suddenly that a cloud I was looking at floated in an immense space, and for an instant my being rushed out, as it seemed, into that space with ecstasy.

The Beat writers saw visions a little more defiantly than Yeats, and involved themselves with language and playfulness of form, and the perception that there are no limits, not even horizons. The Beat writers accumulated influences and models like Yeats (was Kavanagh more original?): the natives Jack London, Henry Miller, Thomas Wolfe; the modernists Proust and Joyce; the Left Bank pundits Sartre, de Beauvoir, and Camus. All of the Beats puttered around in the Twilight Zone, in the bohemian style. Kavanagh was attracted to the *outré* – in a letter to his brother he refers admiringly to that "rascal" Allen Ginsberg.

Bohemia thrived in the mid-1950s in Dublin and San Francisco, though by my day The Catacombs [shebeen in Fitzwilliam Place, Dublin] had gone and The Brazen Head of Beckett had become infested with Royal Irish Constabulary pensioners. Under the high ceiling of McDaid's pub we were in a San Francisco of our own; in a duet between city and author, man and wife, man and woman, man and man. I remember Patrick Kavanagh's declaration of preference for London, which stimulated us, "They don't care who you are or who you're with, they don't ask questions, but mind you it is the same in some ways as here, by the time you get to bed everyone is too drunk to take their clothes off." We began to imagine a Camelot of chandeliers and Scotch.

We got the sense of how comradeship plays out. When Louis MacNeice died, someone suggested Kavanagh write an elegy for that gaunt, edgy Anglo-Irishman, "No, no, but they'll be lonely in London tonight." We lived every day, and I mean day not night, in the enchanted poetry harem of McDaid's – we were caught in a global poetry warming, with a transatlantic ingredient working out the pattern.

We edited a journal, *Arena.* Connections began to abound in this magazine. In our second issue, J.P. Hacket commented in "Aristocracy in Life and Letters", "as to the new generation, Ginsberg and company, well those young men do have a birdlike quality in their flights at times." In our third number, that fine poet Brian Higgins wrote of his first night in literature, "I had just been thrown out of my lodgings and I might just as well go to London as anywhere else. George Barker was in the company, 'Hey, George,' I shouted, 'have a drink.' 'Drop dead, filth,' was his reply." They became the best of friends.

Ireland has always had an underclass who have possessed the leisure for creation and dissent. What was the condition of the bardic order after they were thrown out by the gate lodge onto the bothareen? They licked their wounds in public like Patrick Kavanagh and the Beat writers. There was an eerie quality of repetition here. Let me quote some lines from a poem by Dáithí Ó Brudair ("My Life Has Suddenly Gone Broke"): "This vision in trembling death swoons ditched / clerks and poets, making them paranoid and hungry / in a rough bed, thinking of something terrible to say."

If the Beats are the intellectual elite of dispossession, who don't want a home because you can think better without one, the bards found themselves in the same uncomfortable position. To put it all together, for the Irish poets of the 17th and 18th centuries, for Kavanagh, for Jack Kerouac and Allen Ginsberg, authentic homelessness might be a description of their joint diaspora. Each had another alibi with the future. Their poems or poem-like writings are bathed in the chemistry of people, patrons, local characters, and, more especially, rival poets. There is a gold rush of personal allusion in Beat literature, which is sometimes known as the San Francisco Renaissance.

The Irish Renaissance and the San Francisco Renaissance also share elements of antinomianism. In particular, the force of Kavanagh's poetry agreed with the idea that, unlike the Gospel, the moral law was not binding. Faith in the works of love was sufficient for salvation. Perfect love casts out puritan fear. Kavanagh and Ginsberg were the architects of the victory of love. This concept reflects the bohemian ideal of the lives of the poets, but the Beat writers brought something special to Ireland, a gift described by Leslie Fieldler as "the last, mad effervescence of the dreams of utopian sex". This dream of a revolution against all other revolutions, which for us in McDaid's meant the burial of the inherited backpack of nationalism, overwhelmed us. Now we were at last in America, at last real, living in the present. We ordered more pints as we didn't want to understand our world, we wanted to change it. We needed great personal love, and a bar or a bedroom to celebrate it in.

These were the Irish tremors, the focus suddenly on you, your freedom, your sexuality, the emphasis on song, kiss and dance, and even (within "decent" limits) the orgy. The drinking hours were lengthened, the weekends became festivals, festivals became nights, and the nights became Eire Nua, European perhaps, and maybe also Formorian. The *fleadh cheoils* [music festivals] of the 1960s in Ireland – each became a separate Woodstock. It was no mean achievement to include in our post-Yeatsian heaven, music, writing, conversations, and alcohol. Many men and women of great talent participated in the reawakening. Sean O'Riada, Brendan Behan, Edna O'Brien, J.P. Donleavy – all of these in their ways took part in a Kerouackian dialogue in our minds. The Beat writers, in particular Kerouac, wrote serially, like Joyce and Proust, and my generation accepted this extension of form. Edna O'Brien's first novels offered an alternative sensibility, because they included women in the liberation rituals. I think all of these writers, on both sides of the Atlantic, took up the old idea (Brian Merriman comes into my East Clare mind) that love should be amusing to the point of being funny, but often isn't.

Above all, it was Patrick Kavanagh who led us through the Eisenhower/ De Valera decade. As I knew him, he was bard, but he was also Beat – Beat in ways I am only beginning to think of. In his later verse, which I have always held to be the better part, his poetics is like Kerouac's or Spicer's or Wieners's: flighty, muted, warily innocent, and technically always coming back to spontaneity, the first draft, which is the first law of Beat writing: first thought, best thought. The last five poems in Kavanagh's *Collected Poems,* which I was the first to edit in *Arena,* were a burning out of his previous styles, a liberation into holy ignorance and peace. Kavanagh was and is Beat. Love burns in his language as it does in Ginsberg and Kerouac. If with Yeats the elegiac ecstasy of Poe enters Irish literature via Mangan, then it is with *Come Dance with Kitty Stobling* (Longmans, Green and Co, 1960) that Whitman's "Song of Myself" enters our culture. I buy Kavanagh's words in "America – An Interview":

What do you think of modern American Literature?
Trash.

Any hope for it at all?
Yes. I like those so-called Beat writers like Ginsberg, Corso, Ferlinghetti, and Jack Kerouac.

I like particularly his distinction between men of letters and the fact that "the great works of literature are produced by amateurs, Melville, Swift, Dante, Cervantes, etc." I regard men of letters as being more valuable than Kavanagh's dismissive suggestion, but I know that the aims of these amateurs are very high, and that their concerns are not secular. Mike Wallace asked in an interview with Kerouac:

This Beat Generation has been described as a "seeking generation. What are you looking for?
God. I want God to show me his face.

This strikes me as similar to Kavanagh's desire to find the same face in a cut-away bog. Another aspect of propinquity between these writers is the nature of their rage: the muse of fun and fantasy is also the muse of satire and malice.

In Kavanagh's poetry, I am reminded of qualities I find in Kerouac's *On the Road, Tristessa, Big Sur.* For both Kavanagh and Kerouac have in their language the sparkle of epiphany. This is why they said if the language has this, don't rewrite it.

It is easy to compare sample quotations from interviews with these writers. I'd like to cite Kerouac. "I have to make my choice between all this ['modern literature'] and the rattling trucks on the American road. I think I'll choose the rattling trucks, where I don't have to explain everything, and where nothing is explained, only real." Patrick Kavanagh used to say in McDaid's, "Write about what's in front of you, write about what's on the table."

There was also Kavanagh's answer to a question about that what you have to do in America to put yourself outside the establishment: "To be original and to have a *comic* attitude to life. What you would also want to say to put yourself outside is that Robert Graves and Marianne Moore are of no use." If anything, Kavanagh is darker, more negative, than the Beats.

The legend, which we now unfortunately call public relations, made the Beats stars. They spoke the sparkling liturgies that those of us who dwelt in McDaid's remember. Fame is a beautiful but devastating tune, as Patrick Kavanagh knew, walking through his "streets broad and narrow". My generation saw him orchestrating that music triumphantly. And we heard these extraordinary songs coming from New York, San Francisco, Mexico City, Tangiers. We were pleased and we were conquered. It has all come to roost in what we have done and what we have written.

And it came back to me on January 21st, 1982, when I met Gregory Corso in the Jazz Gallery on the East Side of Milwaukee. Paddy, he said:

> was very sharp. Kavanagh knew he was a poet so he could sit with whom he liked. Oh, he was a good man, a good poet. Him and Brian Higgins, poor fuckers, they made a mistake, they bit the dust, but I'm alive. What a time we had in the Queen's Elm, going with Paddy and Brian to the owner's house [Sean Tracey's, *ed.]* after hours. Those guys owned that man, I'm sure they never paid him, their credit was bigger than his bank account, I'm sure.

And I sat down and wrote to Patrick Kavanagh's widow Katherine Maloney in Rathgar in Ireland all that Corso said, until he was taken off to the smoke-pit by my students. May these "holy barbarians" instruct us from where they are, the starry heavens, their beds.

Me I will throw away.
Me sufficient for the day
The sticky self that clings
Adhesions on the wings.
To love and adventure,
To go on the grand tour
A man must be free
From self-necessity.

– Patrick Kavanagh,
"The Self-Slaved"

The London Magazine (2003)

John Allen Ryan
San Francisco Avatar

I am a poet and my life has been a search for other poets who I could drink with and form a Bohemian world. First I read about these marvelous creatures in literature, then in bars instead of books I met them in the flesh. In this flesh there existed extraordinary momentum, those hands and mouths flow with life.

First forays are local, in first college years I fearfully began adventures in O'Dwyer's on Leeson Street and afterwards in McDaid's on Harry Street. I met professors and students in intense colloquy sometimes crooning over Guinness heads over what happened what might have happened; I set first eyes on the half-filled glasses of the other class the intellectuals: Cruise O'Brien wine-flushed and Racine-lipped, Tommy Woods sledgehammer in *The Irish Times* on Saturdays under the name "Thersites," Dr. Earl McCarthy of Physiology who between purchases for youth showed footnotes relating to his papers in old textbooks – a Stephen's Green version of the doctor in *Nightwood* who was also Irish and plastered.

I lingered long and went down town to Bohemian graduate school on Harry St. I have described in my published memoirs the glittering disarray I met in that palace of high sentence and self-mocking sleaze: all the Olympians in profound states of distress with preliminary drafts of madness, in the mid-anecdotage, on lyric prayer flights that fizzled on paper. It was a convocation of shepherds a parliament of owls, some of them Virgilian, some rustic Gaelic: Paddy Kavanagh, Flann O'Brien, Brendan Behan, John Jordan, Leland Bardwell, Maree Conmee, Pearse Hutchinson, David Franklin, on occasion John Montague and John McGahern, on very rare occasion Wilfred Sheed and Louis MacNeice. A drinking stable, a selection of stable boys, a saloon never known again.

Thence I sailed the airwaves and came to the holy, happy, unholy city of San Francisco where choirs of Bohemians sang me often to an earned rest. Here was a cornucopia elaboration of Dublin, the hills were so steep, the ocean so omnipresent and pier-touching, the cable cars clangorous, that foreigners straightened up and observed the living and the oracular. Jack Spicer, the king of the gypsies if there were any gypsies, the queen of the buccaneers and there were buccaneers and buckeens minor young gentry who needed rare friendship, had just died. Around that grieving fact assembled many printers, publicans and princes, often men left over – but one had to keep out of harm's way from political thinkers like Ferlinghetti or the shadow of numbing men of letters like Rexroth, also being careful to limit dalliance with that razzle-dazzle Robert Duncan as the golden mega articulator popped up in San Francisco State cafeteria or in Mark Linenthal's house after Wednesday's poetry reading.

I sailed on a cable car down Market Street to North Beach and met John Allen Ryan in Gino and Carlo's on Green Street. We fell into each other's drinks, the beginning of all contact.

He was larger than poetry readings, larger than campus people. Had the old Californian pre-war yearning about being just a State and having charm and integrity of a State. He was a cowboy of the Sierras, loved stones, mountains, and trails. Loved dressing up for them with backpacks. Had the American obsession to cook gourmet food. He had been a student at the CSFA, Spicer had been his teacher; he was one of the artists who set up the Gallery Six Reading that set off fireworks: Beatdom, San Francisco poetry. He became Ginsberg's lover in the fifties; if you want a description look up Ginsberg's Journals Mid-Fifties (Allen and I talked about him in The Temple Bar Hotel, Dublin, in the late nineties – the poet frowned at my report that John had AIDS). John's poetry was Whiterabbited, he came to the notice of Ruth Witt-Diament of the San Francisco State Poetry Center. Worked as a bartender in the legendary "The Place" and in a pizza restaurant both on Green Street. He said he was on the wagon from 1974 to the nineties. He moved in with Robert Berg the librarian at San Francisco State who used to empty the shelves of cookbooks and take them home – the story was John hid Berg's quart of gin in the oven to curb thirst, Berg came home and preheated the oven, the gin exploded and there was no cooking (but it could have been the other way round, Berg putting the alcohol in). Chateau life was often difficult in the hilly town.

Two scenes hover in my memory. Graham Mackintosh of White Rabbit, Jim Chapson, John and I in Gino and Carlo's in long lofty intake near the jukebox Spicer tried to plug. We get out to the street, John goes up a way and stops young male pedestrians some in military uniform (Vietnam time) and propositions them. A second's silence then instant and what looks like major recoil. I flee to the end of the block, I improvise exits. Another time Jim and I are sitting in the Berg/Ryan house on Russian Hill, Berg is out. John tells us Berg is threatening to evict him because he says his tenant is bringing home too many men and that reminds him of his mother. John brings down his journal to show us, it is lined in five coloured sections each detailing part of each day's occurrences. The writing is pointed: what a trove of personae and melodies of rage and revenge. Also the complete record of the San Francisco

Renaissance down to last kiss, whisper in ear. I recollect a conversation about druids with John at a party of the old Joe Dunn/White Rabbit boys, Dick Bratset and Berg and others, cavaliers on couches, shrieks behind curtains, discreet camping by the dips.

Thereafter a strong stream of letters and an occasional blizzard of calls, the latter arriving at any time of the day or night in either of my two countries in the manner of sweet Jack Kerouac – beat calls that know neither time, place nor price – interrupting a couch flirtation in Milwaukee or walking in bare night clothes on cold boards in an unheated Irish house listening for half an hour to repetition or poem. One said little, little was required. "I have not been sober since coming back from the last mountain trip. Have been ill since picking up some virus from one of Ronnie Primrack's kids at the Thanksgiving party Berg and I gave for ten people: The Primracks, Pam and Jack Thibaud, Nemi Frost and her paramour Jason, Dick Bratset ... Ronnie had what was said to be an excellent reading at Intersection Union Street. I missed it as I was smashed out with Bobby, but Ron had been here the night before and read most of his better things to me (which I much prefer to public readings). Ron got a standing ovation, Larry Kearney, who also read, did not." The curious thing about John's phone voice was its formality, its oratory, its precision even in the early years when it was not quite steady. One was addressed but in a public way. His letters also had that near perfect open quality, not quite stilted, a proclamation of his life and San Francisco.

John found a friend Terry from Wisconsin who visited us in Milwaukee at Christmas on the way to his folks. They were in love for fourteen years, Terry died of AIDS in 1991. John tried to soldier on, looking for roommates and getting household volunteers. He had great fun telling about one of them, "a 42-year-old farmer from North-West

Ireland, he is taking classes in literature and sociology at USF. He and I spend more time jabbering than vacuuming, he is quite literate, a very good listener as well as talker, a rare combination. I look forward to his weekly visits with glee." On St. Patrick's Day, 1994, John told me he baked "two lovely loaves of Ryan's Cranberry/Orange/Nut Bread, in which I use 1/2 wheat, 1/2 coarse white flour+ 1/2 Turbinado [Mexican Raw Sugar] and a 1/2 coarse white; eggs, leavenings, 3 lg. Navel oranges with grated peel & other such nice things." This was months before the last phone call after I got back from Wexford to Milwaukee. The phone rang, the voice again more formal than ever, informing me he had AIDS (which he'd mentioned before) and was going to commit suicide, that he was going to do it in the mountains, that he had joined the Neptune Society and wanted me to scatter his ashes from a boat in San Francisco Bay. What can a friend do, how much can he argue? I argued but gently. I demurred at the funeral arrangements; I said I was a traditionalist. I said my own Roman prayer over the phone which he didn't listen to.

A curious thing happened this year. On AbeBooks.com a group of eleven postcards of mine written to John between 1970 and 1990, appeared for sale for $675.00. Since they show the way I used talk to him I will quote two of them – from Kenosha for St. Valentine's Day 1973, "Padraic Colum's voice reminds me of the Celtic verse. O my country, we have plenty. Roses are coming. Happy Valentine, James." And from Milwaukee for Christmas 1984, "May there be a message under the Tree which says that J. Christ will be our literary agent in 1985. Happy Folly Days, James."

He once told me proudly that his eight great grandparents were all Irish Protestants. I told him that made difficulties for a toast. Farewell and happiness, son of Reformation Ireland and hedonistic California.

The late Mrs. Witt-Diament
would likely tell her class
that you use rocks and stones
much as Whitman used the grass.

The Blue Canary (2007)

Remembering Nic Kubly

"Nic" Kubly, as I and some of his friends called him, was that now largely unrecognizable type, the Mid-western patrician. He was a heartland seigneur. His land, his house in New Glarus were habitations of public trust. So to speak, he conducted the Wilhelm Tell Orchestra himself.

Like those of us who survive into newer ages he became, malgre lui, a museum keeper. For me, the symbol of his Arcadia time was his '38 Buick, whose beautiful, white tires once ruled the earth. An early summer in the 70's we were in New Glarus for a Swiss frolic; all day some of Kubly's house guests worked on the old Buick which had been kept in a shed for the winter. Slowly it was brought back to perfect working order and fed its gasoline. We filed in, and with Nic at the wheel, we arrived in New Glarus. At the hotel, the car was parked and we were serenaded by yodeling. Wilhelm Tell served us drinks from behind the bar.

I learnt that every few years New Glarus goes to Old Glarus in Switzerland, one of the central meadows of Europe. Nic Kubly wrote the books they read on the plane.

Kubly was our friend, a great traveller whose journals were part of his autobiography. He combined in his best writing, place, fact, elaboration, and absolute timing. He had an equal sense of adventure and evasion about his (the author's) life. He was the good American of the 40's/50's, the good citizen being defined in those days as the non McCarthyite supporter. I think his greatest books were fueled by that protest, the desire to escape from home shores. The steady elegance of his views on democratic citizenship! I think his best books are *An American in Italy,* and *Easter in Sicily;* the former won the National Book Award when there were very few categories. Perhaps one should say: love it and leave it and write about it.

I had good times with Nic in Wisconsin – it was he who brought me here – parties in Racine, restaurant visits to Milwaukee, and weekends in New Glarus. A few things stand out in my memory: the Buick, his friendship with colleague Orph Johnson, the magic moment in the workroom of the farm when he showed me his interesting and erotic correspondence with Carl Van Vechten. But no memory hits me as much as the first encounter with him in San Francisco, on my second day in the New World. It happened on the San Francisco State campus.

There are two desks, one of them occupied. A man in heavy glasses, white and gray sweater, crouches over a pile of manuscripts. He turns to warn me the guy who sat at my desk last semester committed suicide. I bless myself. He introduces himself in a booming voice, "I'm Nic Kubly, you're from Ireland and I'm almost from Europe, I was raised in New Glarus, Wisconsin." He invites me for cocktails to his house on Waller Street that evening. By the time I arrive from downtown into the environs of the Haight Ashbury, he had talked to the landlord of the house next door. There is a condemned basement there I can have. Glasses in hand we go over to see the English-born owner who lives over the basement. I whoopee into the night because I have landed at last.

I walk with Nic Kubly through Golden Gate Park, a massive scene of hippies, love-babbles, and flower children, all sold on magic substances. We go to the museum which has a magnificent Oriental collection. I pause at drawings by Jean Cocteau; there is a sexy one of

Spender simply called "Stephen." We drink jasmine tea in the garden. Kubly tells me his Greek book is finishing; I had been looking over some chapters. (I write real poetry and perhaps non-fiction). Kubly's writing possesses word-density and the power of rhythmical description. We talk about the encroaching "revolution" on campus. San Francisco has embodied for me the ideas of the city as a constellation of poets. Politics, on the other hand, seems a class of earthquake that spills at intervals over this collection of hermetic cells and academic talking shops. Kubly is taking care of the "after shocks" we mention. We always happy-houred.

I have other and perhaps more personal memories of Kubly.

Ghosts, I trust, can come out through the doors of people's ignorances and biases. There is the history of the famous photograph in Spender's coffee table book on Auden. The young Senator John F. Kennedy is presenting the National Book Awards to W. H. Auden, John O'Hara, and Nic. The picture stands forever as a Camelot still. But Nic's story was, "The day after the awards, I was cruising on the New York subway section where you went to pick up guys. I saw Auden, and since I had spoken to him the day before, I approached him. He snubbed me." Or his account at the California dinner table when he woke up among the silverware after taking a nap. He began to enumerate those whom he encountered in New York bath houses in the early 40's. To mutter only of the dead, Leonard Bernstein, and Stephen Spender blissfully still unknighted: Kubly boomed like God the Father or was it Zeus, "Spender's cock was the biggest I had ever seen, it was as thick as a coffee can." The genteel audience perhaps shuddered. But Nic had lived on the coasts as well as in Wisconsin, had refurbished desire.

Perhaps Nic had unusual crystal-gazing powers. Once he said, "You know Thornton Wilder had sex only on trains in Germany." I worried about what Wilder did during 1939–45, but maybe unnecessarily.

I visited Nic last spring, after an interval of many years. I caught him, by divine providence, in his last weekend on his farm. He recognized me, asked me about my sister, we reminisced about San Francisco, and we talked about Kay Boyle, a one-time friend and patron. I brought two ex-students with me, Jerod Schroeder and Tomas Larscheid; we were sitting cozily over his wife's drink when Nic burst out to the two "You're not Swiss." He was as sharp as a cucumber. Wilhelm Tell was still operating. Friendship, of course, is not guilt by association, not even association, it is the coming together of massive forces of coincidence, unity, and affinity. Another farm boy out of the Midwest with moonlight in his eyes and Hermes in his finger tips.

Ave atque vale.

Blue Canary (1977)

TWO

The Double Vision of Irish-American Fiction

Confronted with dual and sometimes conflicting values of Irish and American culture, Irish-Americans are forced to make choices that affect them emotionally, socially, and politically. Different from Irish fiction, which tends to explore subjective reality and to use experimental narrative techniques, as in writers such as James Joyce and Flann O'Brien, 20th century Irish-American fiction is characterized by a dramatic, easily accessible story in which men and women with divided loyalties and sensibilities work out their fate. Irish-American fiction inevitably reflects this conflict and adjustment of values as it identifies the models from Irish and American culture that merge in the self of the consciously Irish American. A separate background can emerge which is distinct in its ethnicity, yet without visible ties to the Irish of Ireland. Who are the Irish-Americans and who are their writers? Irish-Americans are predominantly the Catholic, largely Gaelic, immigrants that came to the United States from the first half of the 19th century to the mid-1950s. This uprooting was caused by racial and political oppression, famine, and poverty. Mixed in appears some voluntary immigration, of an adventurous and practical kind. A much smaller group of immigrants consisted of those of Anglo-Irish or Irish stock, Protestant by faith, who crossed the Atlantic from the 17th century onwards.

The elements of Irish-American authorship remain more conjectural. Mere birth, or descent, from an Irish-American origin seems an inadequate definition. Such writers will bear an ethnic name or background, but no more. It is perhaps hard to know where to draw the line, but I suggest that F. Scott Fitzgerald and Flannery O'Connor, for example, are not Irish-American writers. Their work does not involve itself with Irish or Irish-American themes. An Irish-American fictionist should at a minimum have published a novel, or a number of stories, concerning his ethnic context. Flannery O'Connor, in a recently published letter, explicitly dissociates her craft:

> I have never been greatly tied emotionally or sentimentally to my own Irish background. The Irish in America are sometimes more Irish than the Irish and I suppose some of my indifference is a reaction against that. (Fitzgerald, 531)

Mary McCarthy, by virtue of her *Memories of a Catholic Girlhood,* can be reckoned a partly Irish-American writer. From the first chapter of the book one can gather an impressive list of Irish ethnic character traits: mendacity in the family members, the power of tale telling, romanticism that often hides personal weakness, religious scruples, confessional attitudes, and alcoholism. Over these not quite melted-pot kindred stands the figure of the author's paternal grandmother whose piety "was an act of war against the Protestant ascendency" (33). Her "Old Country" heritage blooms in sentiments like, "The extermination of Protestantism, rather than spiritual perfection, was the boon she prayed for" (34). Many ethnic writers have been lucky in a genealogical look back. Identification, culture, ancestral richness relate to one another in the extended work of other novelists and writers in the Irish-American tradition of letters. In its main line, which at times coincides with "mainstream American" literature, I would place: Jimmy Breslin, James Carroll, Elizabeth Cullinan, John Gregory Dunne, Peter Finley Dunne, James

T. Farrell, Thomas J. Fleming, Mary Gordon, Pete Hamill, Tom McHale, John McNulty, Brian Moore, Edwin O'Connor, John O'Hara, J. F. Powers, Betty Smith, and Harry Sylvester. J. P. Donleavy falls in the category of having reversed the translation across the Atlantic; Eugene O'Neill must be in a category – or hell – all his own. There is also minor side work by WASP writers close to the ethnic context, such as Stephen Crane's *Maggie: a Girl of the Streets.*

A basic factor in this literature is that Ireland and Irish-America became in many respects two distant but related climates. Racial role and memory separated at some point in the last 150 years. Literary fiction is the clearest mirror for what happened. Irish-Americans' versions of Ireland are mostly Arcadian dreams of a vanished Celtic-Christian civilization. In Seán O'Faoláin's novel *Come Back to Erin* a conversation occurs at the outset between the Guard, a member of the Irish police, and St. John Hogan-Hannafey who has spent 34 years building up a business in the New World, "I suppose you never heard of H. H. shoes. Well, I'm the man who makes H. H. shoes. Coast to coast in the United States there isn't a town where you can't buy Hogan-Hannafey Shoes ..." (34). As the English Market clock in Cork rings the half hour, they sum up their philosophies of history, "'Aye!' said the Guard, 'History is wonderful.'" To which the returned emigrant replies, "'Wonderful! But there's an awful lot of it to remember.' "(40). Earlier they had been talking about Charlotte Quay and the Guard challenges St. John as to whom it is called after. When St. John is informed that it is named after a Mecklinburg-Strelitz princess, he bristles. A cultural conflict immediately takes place. "All these are the names of our conquerors and they should be wiped out. We Irish in America can't understand why you haven't wiped them out long ago"(39).

The belief of the Irish-American about Ireland's Golden Age is reflected in the aggressive patriotism of one removed from the country's actual problems. Nationalism, from a distance, lacks understanding and knowledge of the ambiguities of local pieties. The Irishman, not unfairly represented by a member of the new police force, is a realistic traditionalist. His obsession with history does not become enthrallment: he remains intrigued but cynical about his country. Ironically, but logically, the first popular writer of Irish extraction in the immigrant-fed continent was John Boyle O'Reilly, a poet and Fenian who made a daring escape from an Australian penal colony. His once great reputation has vanished.[1] Strength in Irish-American literature from the beginning was concentrated in fiction, and to a lesser extent in drama. This lead was taken by Peter Finley Dunne and his creation, Mr. Dooley, who keeps a tavern on Chicago's "Archey Road." Dunne had in embryo the touch of Swift; he could have collaborated on the Drapier letters. In, for instance, "The Necessity of Modesty among the Rich: a Tale of the Famine" – what flying Swiftian echoes – we get the package description of the Irish agrarian scene. His historical accuracy is linked to his talent in getting Irish-American speech down on paper: through the barely transparent antic mask he was able to cut more deeply than other ethnic writers. He possessed a magic ear; at its best, it seems evocative of an Irish writer, say Sean O'Casey. The endurance of the home tradition is shown in his ability to remember and think in native Irish terms, the most developed of which is comedy.

The Irish immigrants, determined for the most part not to work on the land, built up and expanded urban communities in the major cities. Their intricate sense of rural customs was transformed into street and ward networks. Where they did settle the land, they often found familiar resistance, the shadow of the past, perhaps more plainly than in the cities. J. F. Powers, the most uncompromising writer about the terrifying clericalism of the private Irish-American world, describes the situation at the opening of *Morte D'Urban.*

> Harvey Roche (later Father Urban) was born in that part of Illinois which more and more identifies itself with Abraham Lincoln but has its taproot in the South. Protestants were very sure of themselves there. If you were a Catholic boy like Harvey Roche, you felt it was their country, handed down to them by the Pilgrims, George Washington and others, and that they were taking a risk in letting you live in it ... What troubled them was the hocus-pocus that went on in Catholic churches ... Wasn't it all very strange there, in that place, at that time, the fancy vestments, the Latin, the wine? What if Catholics were Protestants, and Protestants were Catholics, and *they* worshipped in such a manner? What would Catholics think ... He knew, too, that Catholics were mostly Irish and Portuguese, and that their religion, poverty, and appearance ... were all against them. (76–77)

This social disfigurement also pervaded urban immigration; families had fluctuating rhythms of social mobility. James T. Farrell, a most considerable ethnic writer, is witness:

> I am a second generation Irish-American. The effects and scars of immigration are upon my life. The past was dragging through my boyhood and adolescence. Horatio Alger Jr. died only seven years before I was born. "The climate of opinion" (to use a phrase of Alfred North Whitehead) was one of hope. But for an Irish boy born in Chicago in 1904, the past was a tragedy of his people. (*New York Times,* 14)

One perceives at once the hostilities rooted in European history. This was indeed a home like home; its reality is glimpsed in many corners of American literature. At the end of Carson McCullers's *The Member of the Wedding,* Frankie Addams sees her new friend's Catholicism as "a final touch of strangeness, silent terror, that completed the wonder of her love" (151). Ethnic prejudice seems immovably in the past; enforcing of citizenship concepts was obviously motivated by a policy of lessening incompatibilities. Such difficulties, though, were also part of the trial of America's innocence: Alfred Kazin has written alarmingly about a stealthy first visit to a church (17).

Common perplexities remained in the experience of the stay-at-home Irish and the Irish in exile. But divergences appeared in consciousness. Physical environment, new world economics and politics, different principles of living, parted the race like a stock split. There stands more than one kind of Irishry: dissimilar rag and bone shops of the heart proliferate. One change is that Irish-American fiction is not Dionysian, nor in any sense demonic. No single force or frustration takes over the characters. Eros, anger, and rage are muted; the craving for power evokes only political appetites.[2] Irish-America exists as the realm of the domestic imagination – God's and society's. Irish-Americans are clericalist with a vengeance. With them the family achieved status unknown in the loose and flexible arrangements of Connacht or Munster sentiment. A good percentage of this fiction concerns the dispositions of priests. An intense eye is cast on the cloth.

Typical is Thomas J. Fleming's novel *The Good Shepherd,* in which a bishop of Irish descent attempts a Vatican II revolution in his diocese, to the distaste of senior priests and the useless help of liberal, young clergy. Edwin O'Connor's *The Edge of Sadness* portrays a rehabilitated priest who, in the web of his relationship with the wealthy Carmody family, discovers sanity as well as sanctity. Powerful as are O'Connor's penetrations of the ghetto of the Catholic priesthood – his intimations of Irish ward politics in *The Last Hurrah* and his cameo of selfish old age in *I Was Dancing* are just as riveting – they possess no equivalent in Irish literature. Native writers of Catholic fiction are noticeably second-rate, such as the good Canon

Sheehan and the late Richard Power. This occurs in spite of a roughly similar historical position for both groups; the immigrants, with their defensive mentality linked closely to their parish, exalted their priests as heroes – the native Irish had the "halo image" dependence on their clergy in the Penal Law period. O'Connor describes vividly the old style parish in *The Edge of Sadness:*

> One with a fine, big, old fashioned, well-kept church ... with lots of Irish to put inside it. People like ourselves, Hugh. The kind of people you grew up with; the kind of people you like, the kind of people you *understand:* comic, picturesque, a little sharp in the tongue ... (418)

Jimmy Breslin has a more satiric picture of a latter-day parish in his *World Without End, Amen.* How out of step these scenes of rounded belief seem compared to the unflattering realizations of priests and parishes in native fiction: Joyce's acid negatives, Kate O'Brien's simpering official portraits, John McGahern's cells of darkness.

A complaint critics formulate against this pious background is its engagement with sentimentality.[3] The accusation reinforces the impression of the absence of vision in Irish-American writing. Edwin O'Connor lacks a semblance of poetic energy or premonition, though his characterization is finely painstaking and his situations shrewdly conceived. Nothing haunts the language, as is patent on the surface of the native novel. O'Connor was aware of these discrepancies, but not sufficiently so as an artist. The most accomplished American writer on Irish themes has to confront an intolerable, sweetened image of Ireland as a white ethnic Shangri La. It is not easy to keep out the shibboleths: shamrock and shillelagh. The extent to which Ireland is mythologized is demonstrated by a passage from Jack Kerouac's high school novel, *Maggie Cassidy.* Kerouac, an imaginative literalist, can write like this, "– The dark flowing enriched silty heart – Irish as peat, dark as Kilkenny night, sorcerous as elf, red-lipped as red-rubied morn on the Irish sea on the east coast as I have seen it, promising as the thatched roofs and green swards there bringing tears to my eyes to be an Irishman too and lost and sunk inside her forever …" (77). A feeling of limitation about Ireland obviously would serve as release of an esthetic as well as an ethnic vitality.

Later generations of writers take care to do this, either by knowledge of the home culture or by restriction to the Irish-American dimension, with no cross-Atlantic reference. Mary Gordon and Pete Hamill are representative here. Mary Gordon's best selling *Final Payments* contains, in the sketch of the protagonist's father, the rock on which Irish-America felt safe, to the detriment of its creative power. Everyone who resides in this Queens neighborhood has an Irish name and an Irish-American style. The father, whose house the first paragraph tells us is always full of priests, keeps manners more sacerdotal than any cleric and a Roman Catholicity more inflexible than Pius XII.

> He loved the sense of his own orthodoxity, of holding out for the purest and the finest and the most refined sense of truth against the slick hucksters who promised happiness on earth and the supremacy of human reason. In history, his sympathies were with the Royalists in the French Revolution, the South in the Civil War, the Russian czar, the Spanish fascists (2).

This ideological menu reveals Roman Catholicism in the abstract. None of his right-wing causes refers to Irish events or agents: Red Hugh O'Donnell, Daniel O'Connell, Michael Collins, the rosary-laden Eoin O'Duffy, leader of the Irish Blueshirts – to mention the Celtic heroes of the Ultramontane temperament – are passed over. This professor of medieval literature is not a caricature; he symbolizes the Irish-American parish ghetto. In terse but delicately lengthened sentences, from which irony is almost fully drained, the authority is before us which seeded many of the Irish immigrants. The author shows it at odds with intellectual honesty and recalcitrant to emotional innerness, as witness the father's psychotic reaction to the daughter's affair with his student. The church of immigration and ethnic neighborhood is frozen on her pages with a kind of sunset dissolving. J. F. Powers exhibits a similar twilight in the face of totalitarian excess. Mary Gordon's Isobel attempts to ring out the old with new responsibility; it is never quite rung out. If any race is echo-haunted, it is the Irish.

Elizabeth Cullinan has the same astringent eye for Roman folly, but is more ruthlessly open to the demands of truth in fiction than Gordon. She registers as more complexly autobiographical. Her art presents single-shot, slowed-down moments of life in an Irish New York Matriarchy. In her stories the fathers peep forward in shadows, bread losers, happy go lucky, financially distressed: "Her father was in the classic Irish pattern of wit and improvidence, and her mother was classic Irish, too – devout, innocent, good-hearted, fearful, a woman who was never clear in her mind or easy at heart" (80). The protagonists are mainly daughters, consumed by motherly ambition, and beating uncertain paths, like Isobel of *Final Payments,* to love and friendship. Clerical minotaurs abound. One story, "Only Human," describes the grotesque happenings of a Jesuit wake. A few stories are set in Ireland; when we can get Cullinan more in perspective, we will be firmly stationed in the middle of the double vision. There is a difference in her work between being clever and being serious; feelings accumulate about the matter of Irish-America. We become aware of a more sombre tone, of shades that do not pull up, of entrance and origin, and of the mortal tale:

> I thought of the Kennedys in Washington, the Kennedys in London, the Kennedys in Boston and Hyannis Port. Which were the important days? The days in the White House? The

> days at the Court of St. James's? Or had everything that mattered taken place long before, on the beaches of Cape Cod where we saw them sailing and swimming and playing games with one another? (179)

Cullinan writes out of the need to observe the family, yet keep a distance. Mary Gordon's novel stares at the wrack of the institution. Jimmy Breslin's *World Without End* studies the disintegration of the individual inside the family; it provides a close-up of a family that knows Ireland and Irish-America. Dermot, a cop who is in trouble, reminisces about his childhood in Queens, with his uncles who drank. The 1916 Proclamation of Independence hangs on the wall as he goes to the door of the refrigerator for his rice crispies (49). But the warmest-blooded young Irish-American novelist is Pete Hamill, whose Christmas story *The Gift* has been reissued in paperback.

At the inception, *The Gift's* protagonist, also called Pete Hamill, stands on the New Jersey Turnpike with a state trooper. He has been hitch-hiking, and is being put on a Greyhound bus to New York. Back from the bootcamp of the Korean War, he alone is not met at the Port Authority. He makes his way to a poor Irish section of Brooklyn. He carries two obsessions: to get back his irretrievable girlfriend and to discover his father as person and ethnic progenitor. He hangs on until he is able to find communion with his bar-combing father. The novel centers around a stagnant neighborhood; it brings to mind the Chicago South Side of James T. Farrell's *Studs Lonigan.* Farrell was, on both sides of his family, a second generation Irish-American, while Hamill's parents came from Belfast. Both writers require a great amount of dialogue, and the special setting: the alcoholic phonograph. Pete warms himself up through the night with auditory hallucinations of his father's voice from the bar across the street.

> The songs were always about Ireland, about Galway Bay, and the strangers who tried to come and teach us their ways; about Patty McGinty's Goat and My Old Scalara Hat and the Night Rafferty's Pig ran away; about Kevin Barry and the Bold Fenian Men … my father's voice singing there, for strangers and friends, as year faded into year, all years the same, singing about some long-gone green island and his own sweet youth (18–19).

Patrick Lonigan, the father of Studs, drinking to shut out his son's death, sings a different range of ditties: "The River Shannon," "Dear Old Girl," "When I First Met Mary," or "After the Ball Is Over" (808).

Bill Hamill comes from Ireland and knows the music and the feel of the history; with Lonigan, totally Irish-American, it is the occasion, however desperate, for sentimental joys and sorrows. Pete guesses his father left Belfast for more than economic reasons. In the bar, before the beers and the fight they shared together has reconciled them, he asks his father about the IRA:

> He laughed, and I laughed, and we had another round. "What was the old country like?" He looked at me, his eyes wary, and shook his head. "To hell with the old country," he said. (78)

How distant this is from the pious patriotic Irish-American. The character Pete Hamill has real affinity to Ireland, he suggests the figure of Stephen Dedalus. Both desist from Mass and the sacraments. They have affection for younger brothers and sisters and the mother who holds everything together. They dream of travel, Paris, to become artists, creators of consciousness. Dedalus and Hamill seem like brothers. Their fathers, too, behave in similar fashions. Akin to Simon Dedalus's glows the portrait of Bill Hamill in this short fiction, "But I loved the way he talked and the way he stood on a corner with a fedora hat and raincoat on Sunday morning, the face shiny, the hair slick under the hat, an Irish dude, waiting for the bars to open"[24] and, I might add, facing both aspects of a double vision (33–34).

Éire-Ireland (1984)

NOTES

1 He did not survive being Ulysses S. Grant's favorite poet.

2 Nikos Kazantzakis believed "every great people has *its* own bluebird, the supreme and mystical ideal. Ancient Greece had beauty; Rome, the State; Jews, divinity; the Hindus, Nirvana; Christianity, the everlasting kingdom." Nikos Kazantzakis, *England* (New York, 1965), p. 280. In this scale of imponderables Ireland has the verbal imagination.

3 See Ronald J. Dunlavey's review of *The Last Hurrah* referred to in Hugh Rank, *Edwin O'Connor* (New York, 1974), pp. 89-90, For a contrary view see Edmund Wilson, *The Devils and Canon Barham* (New York, 1973), p. 120.

WORKS CITED

Breslin, Jimmy. *World Without End, Amen.* New York: 1973

Cullinan, Elizabeth. *Yellow Rose*. New York: 1977.

Farrell, James T. *Studs Lonigan*. New York: 1977.

Fitzgerald, Sally. ed, *The Habit of Being*. New York: 1979.

Fleming, Thomas J. *The Good Shepherd*.

Gordon, Mary. *Final Payments*. New York: 1978.

Hamill, Pete. *The Gift*. New York: 1973.

Kazin, Alfred. A *Walk in the City*. New York: 1951.

Kerouac, Jack. *Maggie Cassidy*. New York: 1978.

McCarthy, Mary. *Memories of a Catholic Girlhood.* New York: 1957.

McCullers, Carson. *The Member of the Wedding*. New York: 1975.

The New York Times, August 23, 1979, Sect. B., 14.

O'Connor, Edwin. *The Edge of Sadness*. Boston: 1961.

… *I Was Dancing*. New York: Bantam, 1965.

… *The Last Hurrah*. New York: Atlantic Monthly Press, 1956.

O'Faolain, Seán. *Come Bath to Erin.* London: 1940.

Powers, J. F. *Morte D'Urban.* New York: 1962.

Croesus and Dorothy Day: *Moon Gaffney*'s Irish America

The passion of Ireland is to talk about people when they are alive; the passion of North America is to discuss people when they are dead, but only on family trees. On the one hand gossip, on the other hand genealogy. In *Moon Gaffney*, one of a number of decisive novels of the late 1940s to mid-1950s, Irish Americans can be seen to do both. The other energy of this group is to carry war against its designated enemies. Because it is New York, the characters are more Irish-American than the Irish Americans themselves so they shoot from the trenches of a militant New World. With their version of the United States as protector, they intend to give no quarter to contemporary opponents. To get at what the novel is trying to do, perhaps I can rephrase my favourite Jacobite Dr. Johnson – patriotism is the last refuge of immigrants and possibly for several generations. The patriotism of this community holds two double swords: one combining church and state; the other, two Atlantic coasts.

I can record two surprising footnotes about Sylvester's *Moon Gaffney* (1947). It was written in Guatemala City. While working on this paper in the University of Wisconsin-Milwaukee's Jeremiah Curtin Hall, I discovered that its author, the Brooklyn writer Harry Sylvester, was the grandson of Jeremiah Curtin (1835–1906) – Lincoln's polyglot consul in Moscow, first scholarly collector of Irish folktales. Surely an irony here: an Irish-American model and mentor and a descendant who uses satirical fiction to dissent from ethnic pieties.

My strategy in identifying the renegade nature of *Moon Gaffney* involves a few heresies of my own, including personal genealogy, that dash of soothsaying proper to a bard and critical commentary. For one of the characters in Harry Sylvester's novel, the most complete villain in fact, is based on a cousin of mine, Eddie Reeves, here called Peter Calahan. There is a lot of non-fiction in the book. Dorothy Day – one of the good people, rather I should say saints, in the plot – appears under her own name. An appearance by Al Smith, recorded as "honest Al", turns into a self-conscious hymn for Irish America. That paean gives a glint of light in the grim portrait of the ruling powers of the city of New York – here termed "The Hall", otherwise Tammany – that political machine that lived, according to Steven Erie, by "the trading of divisible benefits ... [and] provided loaves and fishes for its followers" (Clark, 43). Sylvester's method is a glance-by-glance, chat-by-chat, denunciation-by-denunciation, innuendo-by-innuendo demonstration of what it takes to keep and increase power in an atmosphere of plush assimilation rituals and folk snobberies. Yet Sylvester sings, too, of the Emerald re-creation of New York, surely an accomplishment of triumphalism and symbol of the deliverance dreamed of by the Gaelic poets under colonialism.

By moving through several groups of characters at various high social levels, *Moon Gaffney* details this new world of riches. The glittering pageant revealed is a different parade from Mr. Dooley's patch of society. As described by Charles Fanning, Finley Peter Dunne offers "solid and sympathetic characterizations of the common people – the labourers, dray man, and mill workers who make up the working-class immigrant clientele of Mr. Dooley's saloon" (21). Sylvester's fourth novel is set in the

1930s. It gives an unmasked view of the networking, racism, and pious fantasies of a society whose original native conditioning supplied only the start of its power. The rebels are the children of a new upper class who seek and deal with crises of conscience. Beside Moon, the reluctant self-examiner, these avatars for justice include his friends James Kavanagh, the more radical Bart Schneider – whose mother is Irish, hardly good enough – and their girlfriends. Their conflict lies with the umbilical "Hall" and Chancery.

The younger males graduate from Notre Dame or Georgetown, where Calahan makes the decision not to enter the family grocery business. Old and young perform their duties on Sunday – even those inclined to anarchism or communism (the decent guys); the sexes smoke; politicos and their friends eat steak in Italian restaurants; the folks drink as much as my great uncle Paddy Reeves, who said on his death bed, "Thank God, I drank enough alcohol to float the *Queen Mary*". Paddy had spent most of his life in New York. The good complain about the Pharisees in the Chancery; the majority keep naming "Commies"; the about-to-get-married can be sure of honourable sex shortly.

My mother's paternal uncles and their children lived on or near Central Park. Their social lives were spent in establishments like the Athletic Club. My great uncle James, the wealthy brother of Paddy, also appears in *Moon Gaffney*. Here I will simply align to Sylvester's text part of James's 1935 message to my mother:

> … Business conditions here are very bad and not a bright spot on the horizon. Labor and government are in firm control and capital is the big bad wolf whom the place is blamed on for the loss of $50 a week jobs they had promised themselves.

The next year James apologized for a "small present" of $100, because Roosevelt was ruining the country. For an account of the brothers and sisters remaining in Scariff,

County Clare, consult Edna O'Brien's short story "The Savages".

The other elitism at work here is exclusiveness in the rectory, in the chancery, in the archbishop's house, in all the environs of St. Patrick's, in the Irish-American clergy and in the "FBIs", or Foreign-Born-Irish priests. Careers in the Catholic church and urban politics were the avenues of upward mobility and assimilation into the American mainstream. These highways were Jansenist highways. A sly omniscient narrator, Sylvester puts into his characters' dialogue and interior monologues historical explanations such as the connections of the all-Ireland seminary at Maynooth with pre-revolutionary France. *Moon Gaffney* is as much a Catholic novel as it is an Irish-American one, for it is a tract that displays an obsession with Roman Church liturgy and routines. As the prologue to Sylvester's *John Fury* explains, they brought their priests with them.

The elders of "The Hall" profess themselves worried by the emergence of "Commie"-type liberalism among young clerics, especially in the supposedly "red" diocese of Brooklyn, which pays some attention to papal encyclicals on labour. Sylvester's ambivalent central character, Moon, who is slowly growing an independence that endangers his position in machine politics, has to visit Hennessy, the court clerk of Brooklyn, to plead with him to send his daughter back to her husband, who represents a left-wing labour union. Though Moon is the son of the deputy fire commissioner, who is a friend of Hennessy, he suffers a rant:

> Our diocesan paper! That ignorant little sheet, run by young twirps of priests ... If you read the nonsense in it, the pure, vicious nonsense. Stuff that came to them from some Communist front organization. The same sort of thing that Roosevelt has started to do. Ah, if ever a man betrayed his supporters, betrayed good Irish hearts, he's the one. (143)

The long walk to the Republican suburbs has begun.

The young priest in the Catholic Worker house, incidentally incardinated in the Brooklyn diocese, Fr. Shanahan, exposes his situation:

> Monsignor Clancy has already requested my removal to another parish ... I am, he says, a radical, a Jew-lover, a complete fool ... he attributes much of my recalcitrance in having been born in this country, to being what he calls an Irish-American. If I were real Irish like him, born in Ireland, I would not have such outlandish ideas (124–25).

The older priests are made of immigrant seminary steel. They dispense no mercy. The Gaffney family pastor Fr. Malone uses the wake of the deputy fire commissioner to press ideology:

> My purpose in this brief talk is to let you know that Communism's enemies not only exist but are themselves militant, not only in Europe where the great Mussolini has cast down the gauntlet, but in this very country ... (202).

Fr. Coughlin had many brothers.

The essays in Casey and Rhodes's *Irish-American Fiction* (1979) contain scant reference to Harry Sylvester, though he is included in the long bibliography. William Shannon's *The American Irish* does not appear to consider him. There appears to be neglect here, considering that the field is not so very crowded. On the other hand Larry McCaffrey, a thorough-going historian, provides trenchant comments on *Moon Gaffney* in his *Textures of Irish America* (1992). If I do not agree fully with McCaffrey, then maybe it is because I am less close to immigrant experience. I regard the provocations of *Moon Gaffney* as seminal and particularly constructive in the sociological context of the religious rigidity of Irish America. *Moon Gaffney* contains the repugnances always available in Irish-American fiction, but here directed at the excesses of a ruling class self-consciously forgetful of its immigrant origins. Sylvester's novel also is a vehicle for an updating of the effects of assimilation into American life.

I like the rhythm and flair of Sylvester's writing as well as the novel's anti-decorative message, which is protected from protesting too much by the clarity of Sylvester's portraiture. The energizing satire of the writing modifies, I think, the "frivolous" and "cruel" aspects of social relations in the novel that McCaffrey finds. There is a good deal in McCaffrey's comment on the courting rituals – "Alcohol is not a substitute for sex" – though there is a description of mature flirtation between Moon and Rosemary Danaher, whose father is also a commissioner (McCaffrey 63–73). Rosemary is a conservative socialite. The most sympathetic woman in the fiction, Ellen Doarn, holds her own against the toadying of her boyfriend Peter Calahan.

Ellen shines in the panorama of the affluent, spiritually inert society around her, typified by the two priests who try to talk her back into the broken engagement with Calahan. One of these is Father O'Driscoll who maliciously gives wrong advice about the rhythm method of birth control to girls at Mount Murphy. McCaffrey mentions him as representative of knavish priests in Irish-American fiction. In general, Sylvester's sketches of priests are less lugubrious than most others in Irish-American fiction, even if not as well crafted as those of J. F. Powers.

Sylvester's picture of the church is even-handed. Ellen goes to see Mount Murphy's Mother Thomas Moore for advice about resisting the clerical enforcement of her marriage. The reverend mother, who stands in for progressive Catholicism, disposes of Father O'Driscoll as if he were a wet tea rag:

> We had him here for a while and since then he's been chaplain of an athletic club, a professional addresser of communion breakfasts and I don't know what else. I wonder he ever gets round to saying Mass (234).

The strength of Sylvester's stance on the church is that it presents both sides of the coin – that which belongs to "The Hall", and that which belongs to the Gospels.

Mother Thomas Moore enacts the contemplative side of radical Catholicism, reflecting for instance on the structural flaws of women's colleges, "We have too many girls come to us for the wrong reasons as it is … I think we even teach sometimes for the wrong reasons …" (20). The circle around Dorothy Day – Linford Thomas, Ed Galvin, and others – deals with practical problems of protesting, feeding, and housing in reaction to such events as evictions from the archdiocese's slum property. Allegories of good and evil are underlined amid the ward and office ramifications of Irish new world empire and new found new world Irish Church. Sylvester throws Dante's *Inferno* and Butler's *Lives of the Saints* into the cauldron of stellar upward mobility. It is plain that Dorothy Day, embattled by the legionnaires of formulaic religion, is the eminence presiding over this morality tale. And against Dorothy Day Sylvester enlists my own cousin, Eddie Reeves, not only as the "heavy", the Croesus, but also as the ultimately spurned fiancé of Ellen Doarn:

> "You don't suppose that Doarn girl's really engaged to that stuffed shirt?"
> "Why not?" Moon said cheerfully. "If you had what he had, she'd be engaged to you, too."
> "What's that?"
> "About half the tea in China," Moon said.
> "Oh, come, come," Kavanagh said. "His folks own a grocery chain. That's all." (20)

Those stores had eight hundred branches before they were sold to Safeway at the period the novel was written. Two farmboy brothers from County Clare built them up. The child of one of them, Eddie's sibling Dan, went on to own the Cincinnati Reds and the Los Angeles Rams and suffer football's first strike from his coach George Allen. Their father, James, had other distinctions. He served on the committee of wealthy Irish Americans who gave Yeats an income in old age. He supplied the funds for Joseph Campbell's Fordham chair. And he showed my mother a first edition of *Ulysses*. Despite his shabby appearance in *Moon Gaffney*, James Reeves did the state of letters some service.

May Saint Dorothy Day pray for them.

New Hibernia Review, 7:1 (Spring, 2003), pp 9–13.

WORKS CITED

Clark, Dennis, "Organizing in America", *The Irish Literary Supplement,* Spring, 1989, 43.

Fanning, Charles. 'Finley Peter Dunne and Irish-American Realism', in Daniel J Casey and Robert F. Rhodes (eds), *Irish-American Fiction* (New York, AMS Press, 1979), 21.

McCaffrey, Lawrence, *Textures of Irish America* (Syracuse, New York, Syracuse University Press, 1992).

Sylvester, Harry, *Moon Gaffney* (New York, Holt, 1947).

ARE THE DISTANT HILLS SO GREEN?
REAL IMAGES OF HOMECOMING IN IRISH-AMERICAN LITERATURE

The child that emerges from his mother's womb does not worry about his origins. For the first few years, attention is concentrated upon parents and surroundings, then upon friends, the tribe or the community. It is only gradually that one becomes interested in religion, history, genealogy or folklore. And it is only after having gone round these questions that the one regarding origins begins to take shape. The past then appears at the tiny tip of his Prussian nose: "Tell me about how I used to be." Aesthetically speaking, such a quest is a pleasure, even if the awakening is difficult. But politically, and in terms of the relocation of individuals, memories are just so many scars, and it becomes impossible to regain the original site. Animosities, which are fundamentally racial, transform events. Whoever becomes aware of the wounds of history in the depths of his soul, inherits a collective unconsciousness made up of stereotypes, clichés, images and contradictions. Lost in the labyrinth of the tortuous events of the past, the thinking victim often finds comfort only in art. The call to arms is transformed into a call to art.

It is thus that upon leaving Ireland, one of the richest countries in terms of memory, I entered into that immense human receptacle that is the United States of America. To my great surprise, I was not disoriented: my mother was born in Far Rockaway (the "Irish Riviera," as they call it there), on Independence Day in 1910, of immigrants from County Clare who had met each other in New York. Upon my arrival, I therefore had connections, a certain perception, a certain sense of what I would be confronted with, and of what I would be able to count upon. But in crossing New York State to arrive at Binghamton University, I began to experience the strangeness of this vast and misshapen America. Discussions with Professor Louis Bolle, with whom I shared a house in 1969, later awakened in me the desire to explore my surroundings, near and far. Louis Bolle enthusiastically enlightened me about the fundamental differences that exist between Europe and North America, differences which are particularly noticeable to an intellectual of French origins. The abandonment of cities and streets in favor of the suburban house with a garage was particularly bothersome to my friend, who went so far as to speak of "syphilis" in describing the cultural void of Binghamton. As for myself, having yet only a slight acquaintance with this new reality, my point of view was perhaps more neutral. But I knew, in the depths of my Celtic soul, that there were many shades of green. And thus, I was the son of my father.

"The green of the distant hills is more green." Nothing illustrates as well as this old saying, born of the population movements and individual voyages, the weight of places left behind and the nostalgia that they evoke. Distance, which implies the point of no return but also provokes at the same time the sum of searing images from the past, is a true source of enchantment. Exiles and emigrants are as though enveloped, bewitched by the aura, often superficial, which emanates from a past which is unchanged because it was lived in another place. This reductionist vision is further reinforced, sometimes by age, sometimes by the occultation of one's own feelings within the family history, tendencies which both reflect a sense of the past that is scarcely faithful to the world – or to the place – as it really is. From a psychological viewpoint, these attitudes may be part of a desire to return to one's mother and to her original protection. But the respect and rhetorical loyalty that the uprooted individual vows to his race or his origins often overflows as well into pious, soothing conventions which risk enclosing him in a narrow, even scornful, vision of what he has just inherited.

The green of the distant hills may have neither the color of life nor that of the green grass: a partial or non-historical view situates there the racial hatred, militarism, forms of social or political risk-taking, or even the vision of an artificial pastoral society. Even when artists, writers, and intellectuals – emigrants or descendants of emigrants – deal directly and profoundly with their country and culture of origin, they must beware of the pitfalls of "tribal revisionism" described above. They must make an effort to escape an excess of emotionalism or any feelings leading to ethnocentrism in regard to the land across the waters.

Those who write ethnographic works on the "good old homeland" must have a personal experience of it, or have analyzed it in good faith. Too often, distance embellishes its subject. When one studies Irish-American texts – probably the most well-established ethnic literature in North America – which talk about the "fucked-up old country," one is constantly bumping into such questions. For the Celtic countries above all, the past is a minefield of false ethnological information. A fiery imagination is a fine thing in poetry, but an awful thing when it is accompanied by impressionistic or atmospheric distortions. Turning round an expression in regard to Irish-Americans, one might say that "Irish-Americans ran the risk of becoming more American than the Americans." They remained "objects" in the process of assimilation, without yet being equal to the task of becoming true "subjects" at the heart of the stratifications of world history.

It is somewhere along that line (impossible to say precisely where, since a logician or a computer cannot approach these seismic cracks) that the voyage home begins. And it is like a spring-tide: the soul of the immigrant awakens; his spirit becomes once more "ancestral." He begins by testing himself, with the command to go off in search of himself (a quest that is part of American romanticism, of which one is again aware when having crossed the border). At first this quest, whether it be sudden or slow, has few variations: what one desires is to fly again home. It is the "immigrant's gap," one which is often the gap of one or several generations. James Markham describes this state of affairs quite well in another racial context:

> In Spain, the people of Gallego are thought to be a sentimental lot, given to sharp pangs of morriña or nostalgia, if they have left its mist shrouded hills, as so many have, to seek their fortunes elsewhere. In this, they have much in common with their neighbors the Portuguese, and with the Irish. Poverty drove many to Latin America and, at the turn of the century, possibly half of all Spaniards crossing the Atlantic were Gallegos. (64)

The word "roots," which Markham employs in the title of his article, does more than pay homage to fashion. For the need to find that which has been lost, with the physical transformation of one's offspring into citizens of another country, surfaces anew. A process of "detransformation" attempts to see daylight and the anthropologist exhausts himself in rediscovering the traces of an identity and a way of life.

The numbers relative to Irish immigration are eloquent. Between 1845 and 1855, the number of Irish "boat people" arriving in the United States was around a million and a half. Between 1855 and 1870, there was another million, and again a million and a half between 1870 and 1900. In 1860, in the American population, 5.12% were citizens of Irish origin. The Census of 1980 indicates that more than forty million Americans are of this descent, and among those, ten million are of pure Irish stock. Ethnic character became a very important aspect of American individual and family life during the 1970s. Here are some answers about the reasons behind this ethnic "explosion," given to me recently by my students in a course on Irish-American literature: ethnic character gives a sense of the past, a feeling of belonging; it confers cultural identity and security; it compensates for the disappearance of neighborhoods and the appearance of suburbs; it satisfies the need to legitimize a socio-cultural milieu; it produces a feeling of pride and is a good subject of conversation. A small number of students complained that the subject was not viewed with enthusiasm by their families.

It was perhaps the "luck of the Irish" that their first great writer, Peter Finley Dunne, author of the *Mr. Dooley* series, was capable of building a bridge between the two cultural spheres. Born in Roscommon, Mr. Dooley, the tavern-keeper of "Archey Road" in Chicago, is capable of both keeping an ear open to the American scene, and of putting his compatriots on alert: this is a foreign culture, he says, it's not always rosy and it's often hard when for help of any kind, you have to count upon a language that often masks your thoughts, a language in which your quick wits get entangled. Through the setting of a working-class tavern, Peter Finley Dunne becomes a sort of philosopher-humanist, in the vein of the best of Mark Twain. Behind his jester's mask, he says more, while comforting his people, than any other ethnic writer of his day. The success of the *Mr. Dooley* series stems from the talent of its author. He knew how to put the Irish-American dialect on paper, a new pidgin language born of the recent appearance of English in the west, north, and south of Ireland. Dunne cannot avoid parody, but he knows how to combine borrowed words, a mixture of the Irish brought over on the boats, with the linguistic models of the Midwest. Although he was part of the first generation of Irish-Americans, he was nevertheless capable of keeping his ear open to the richness of the language of Irish immigrants in Chicago.

In a lovely preface to one of his novellas, *John Fury*, published in 1946, Jack Dunphy describes the extremely painful integration of these New World waifs:

> Tugged up as they were from their home roots. Plodding up and down gray city streets. Mixing cement, guiding steel girders, digging coal, baking bricks and carrying them. Riding their first streetcar. Jumping at the sight of the first automobile. Tugged up from their home roots, taken and going willingly from the sea smell and peat smells. Taken from their priests and bringing with them only to die on city pavements the love and hatred and blind acknowledgement they gave to priestdom. Shoved into a boat and with sweating and cursing and stinking and praying, with deaths and births, with old age and youth, they landed and a shovel was placed in their hands or a hammer or spade and they built Boston and New York and Chicago and Philadelphia. And in the evenings they walked home in the leaning shadows of the gray stone to their one room or two rooms and fell into bewildered sleep.

The crude images of reality take the place of Epinal's images of "green hills," the odors of peat for those of the sea. The green grass becomes steel, coal, cars. From this violent contrast will be born a series of contradictory images.

Here we are now, confronted with the phenomenon of the "image of going back.". The reality of the good old things of our origins is hidden from us. Only the beauty of the countryside persists, or the tender customs of that place, while the political domination is amplified, that which was often the reason for the exodus. With a writer like Dunphy, one feels the desire to make way for reality. The artificial charm of the past is forbidden (as suggested, in the passage that I just cited, by the term "religious faith") and the first days spent in the adopted country are described with objectivity.

An Irish-American writer who was both realistic and sentimental, Jim Tully, whom H.L. Mencken compared to Gorky, tries to stay as faithful as possible to reality in novels that go against the mainstream. In *Shanty Irish*, he confers upon the immigrant's memory an authentic virginity. Hughie Tully, the patriarch, is presented to us through a brilliant monologue on the dramas experienced by his forbears:

> "You must have had a lot of fun in Ireland when you were a kid," I said to him.
> Grandfather looked at me. And then at his glass.
> "There was niver any fun in Ireland, me lad – it was always a wailin' and a weepin' country. Hearts full of the great sadness and stomicks empty of food – fools prayin' to God, and starvin' on their knays." (1–2)

Tully wants to demystify the image of the immigrant, turned nostalgically towards his past. At the beginning of the book, Hughie, who seems to want only to tell the story of the central character, ends up giving a very black view of the facts:

> "What a band of liars an' brigands we Irish are. We'd cut the Pope's throat for a nickel an' burn 'im in hell for a dime. There was only the one trouble with the Great Famine – it didn't starve enough of thim. An' thim that lived through it didn't live. They died an' come to life again. An' yere niver the same once ye rise from the dead – somethin' has gone out ov the heart o' ye. (3)

This voice gives a veritable elegy for the race, all the while manipulating the truth in a language of which only the Irish have the secret. The paradox is rhetorical and the resurrection of the righteous is only the resurrection of that which is possible.

The Irish-American authors who followed Tully's generation, two generations after Dunne, wanted to follow physically in the paths of their ancestors. It was not sufficient for them to give new life to the conversations of their grandparents or parents. They wanted to go see for themselves, to tread with their own feet upon the Promised Land that had been abandoned. They would not be satisfied with conjectures. The Irish-American writer who was probably the most ingenious and the most committed is James T. Farrell. Born in Chicago, he is the author of the famous trilogy, *Studs Lonigan*. He gives examples of returning that seem like encounters with the green prairie. He also wrote five short stories centered on the O'Neill-O'Flaherty families in which he appears autobiographically in the guise of Danny O'Neill. In one of these stories, Danny promises that when he grows up, he will return to Ireland, "'Mother, when I am a man I'm going to get some fairies and I'm going to go with them and fix those landlords in Ireland who are so mean,' Danny said." (*A World I Never Made* 52) Similar sentiments are expressed by Tully's protagonists. Farrell notes that "our forbears partook little of the great culture of mankind. Their lives and destinies were hard; their contributions to our civilization were made with their backs. We have come from their poverty. We have a personal past different from the past suggested in the great and inspiring world of culture and ideas" (*Reflections at Fifty* 10).

Farrell had more leisure time, more choices than the generations who preceded him. He could go see for himself, and what he saw confirmed, beyond all expectation, his dialectical approach to history. He realized that "misery" had always existed or that at least it had appeared centuries before, with the crumbling of the

Gaelic civilization. As a writer of fiction, he definitely had a limited register, and was never capable of expressing a vision of the world that went beyond the Chicago of his youth. But in letters published recently, he analyses his own return: Ireland appears like "an outpost of western civilization. It is little interested anything beyond this green isle. Its intellectuals are little interested in what goes on beyond the bordering seas ... The Irish are deficient in certain sensory capacities. What they do with food is something that resides among the mysteries. Their public statues are beyond imagining."(*On Irish Themes* 162–63).

In one who, in America, feels like a son of Old Ireland, the desire for return is nourished by a series of images that complete the tableau.

An entire generation of Irish-American authors – since this category sometimes penetrates the mainstream of American fiction – has walked in the steps of Farrell, in pilgrimage to the Ireland of yesterday and of today. But unlike him, they have done it through fiction, and their relatively fruitful efforts (often even in the commercial sense of the term) have closed the gap which separates the two Irelands. It seems that now, at least in words, there is an island that floats in the middle of the Atlantic, accessible from both sides.

Jimmy Breslin carried out a return that he describes in his novel *World Without End, Amen*. He tells the story of a young alcoholic policeman from Queens, who gets in trouble because of violent acts and who goes to Ireland both as punishment and for his salvation. Dermot Davey has been uprooted and taken advantage of, tied to Ireland since his childhood, "Dermot went over to the refrigerator to get the milk for his Rice Krispies. On the wall alongside the refrigerator was the Proclamation of Irish Independence of 1916. Everybody in the family, the uncles first of all, had Dermot memorize it" (54). The second part of the book tells how Dermot was taken up, rather passively, in the turmoil of rebellions and counter-rebellions that were already beginning to agitate Northern Ireland. Breslin uses his journalistic sense very well here, mindful of detail and nuance: one rediscovers the lost green country, a country in gestation seen from the Irish-American angle.

More intimate and more bitter is the etching by Pete Hamill, who speaks to us in *The Gift* of his parents and his childhood in Belfast. He succeeds in the tour de force of reconstituting an ancestral memory, and making it credible thanks to the father of the protagonist, Bill Hamill, who knows the soul and the music of the old country. The sensibilities clash when, like a cry from the soul, the son asks the question about the "green":

> "What was the old country like?"
> He looked at me, his eyes wary, and shook his head. "To hell with the old country," he said. (78)

A phrase which echoes the references of Tully and of many another on the Hibernian Way.

In conclusion, here is another example of the "Yankee's return" to the country. This expression can add to the confusion because it evokes both the voyage, in its lyrical serenity, and the vision of the Irish-American writer who is seeking his soul, his identity. As shown by the novels and short stories of Elizabeth Cullinan, these two perceptions are not incompatible. Thus it is that two stories in her collection *The Time of Adam* take place in Ireland and evoke the relations between emigrants and natives. In "Mama's Friends," the female narrator, who is none other than the author, is obsessed by differences which, even though they may be entertaining, do not always amuse her, "Were they making open fun of her or did they think she considered herself in on the fun? It was baffling, but then Ireland itself was more or less that for Cecilia Bell, a problem she brooded about endlessly ..." (160). In "A Sunday like the Others," the woman named Frances has, during a weekend, a totally unsatisfying liaison with a local, narcissistic "new novelist." In the course of her disappointments, she will end up by taking stock of everything that separates them, the strange gaps that are occasionally impossible to overcome, and the first one was during the bus trip to the writer's small house, at the foot of the mountains of Dublin. She imagines that the bus driver thinks she's a foreigner, "Something she herself was always forgetting and, one way or another, always being reminded of. Here in Ireland she was American, though back in Boston she was what was known as Irish. Irish-American." (119)

These two words show clearly that the green hills are nearby: one never ceases to walk round them. Ireland, beware, the Diaspora is watching you!

Marges et Exils, L'Europe des literatures déplacées (1987)
Translated from the French by Jeanne Morgan Zarucchi

WORKS CITED

Breslin, Jimmy. *World Without End, Amen*. New York: Penguin, 1973.

Cullinan, Elizabeth. *The Time of Adam*. Boston: Houghton, Mifflin, 1971.

Dunphy, Jack. *John Fury*. New York: Harper, 1946.

Tully, Jim. *Shanty Irish*. Kent, Ohio: Black Squirrel Books, 2009.

Farrell, James T. *On Irish Themes*. Philadelphia: University of Pennsylvania Press, 1982.

... *Reflections at Fifty*. New York: The Vanguard Press, 1954.

... *A World I Never Made*. New York: The Vanguard Press, 1954.

Hamill. Pete. *The Gift*. New York: Random House, 1973.

Markham, James. "Castro's Roots in Spain." *New York Times Magazine*. 18 November 1979, 64.

DIASPORA ADDENDUM

Not to be self-important or anything, but I have been an emigrant, an exile, a disappearing act, and object on the horizon since 1967 when I left Dublin. I came out of a literary and alcoholic city-culture at its most swan-songish and worked in a succession of North American cities – San Francisco, Portland, New Orleans, and Milwaukee. The first of these drank as much as Dublin and had as many useful poets but not the same quality of bars except North Beach, while Milwaukee suggests Dublin without the same quality of poets but with the bars. I have been in Wisconsin since 1975 and sometimes on rainy afternoons my new city reminds me of my old, though not as much as Chicago which has Irish faces in the rain. Milwaukee can strike me as being as stodgy and as melancholy as Grafton Street in 1955 but with the exception that the former is more erotic; young America seethes as an artificial paradise of desire, at least in the head. To advance temptation, or perhaps just fantasy, the bars close some hours later. As I stand in the music of the last call I am the same writer I would have been in Dublin yet I get the impression my stance looks more sensual.

Maybe it is mostly illusion: I gaze into the mirror; I am an exile, I am not an exile. "Exile" has enough alienation in it to be a real condition yet it often can be read as part of the flashy supernaturalism of the Irish literary tradition. It could mean this, however; the artist type is away from family and friends so cannot be readily interrupted. Distance becomes the spark of reverent memory; writing can seem the activity of alcoholic and workaholic ghosts. The famous like Joyce, Wilde and others used new domicile and café in a more exuberant mode than they would have in Ireland. Our circumstances are more modest, but do not dismiss the soldiering in foreign fields. And my reading list in the US has been different. If I had stayed, would I ever have heard of Lorine Niedecker, Jack Spicer and John Wieners?

My generation heaves out of Modernism and the ambivalence of travel and resettlement is inbuilt. Fragmentation and collage are stamped in our passports. Should I declare myself an emigrant? Changes in Ireland have come so fast that I do find them enchanting. Your Ireland is dead, that clarifies the mind.

If the new emigration is not like the old exile, perhaps I appear in the twilight zone between them. Maybe both are just a reworking of the Joycean formula, have I ever left? For one, I wonder if anyone can ever leave the pre-Vatican II Church. You can see the spire from your window. Montague's words which introduced me to Cavafy first in the old *Bell* moved me unbearably in my McDaid's gilded youth: you grow old in the same city wherever you voyage, your hair whitens in the same street. The dreams and images of the past are possibly more full of vivid light, spectral rain, if you are physically sundered from mother, hedge, and river.

On advantage of *abroad, overseas,* is to be able to play with the matter of Ireland. You can camp it up or at the very least force it into unfamiliar patters. Recently I have been writing epitaphs for myself, and I seem to compose them easily about Dublin. History runs completely as I look back.

In mother's womb I sipped
the elixir of nationalism and words.

Her boyfriend in her mind Yeats
gave me rhythms, Joyce sent invocation,
Ginsberg bestowed liberation.
In Hodges Figgis the City Lights books:
I was devoured by *Howl*, I began
hyperventilating. Bars of Dublin
turned into jammed paradises
with wandering disheveled starlets.

Metre (1998)

Pretexts, or Notes in the Stilly Night

As a two-bit Oisín who decamped from Shannon Airport (brain drain or brain damage?) hires a big horse to ride into the incredible past of Irish poetry, my views on its contemporary state are perhaps general and dated. Once I was in the thick of the plumed smoke: the sweltering of the sixties. Now I am puzzled by Irish poetry's in-dwelling, its lack of energy in the creation of different voices, and its armourclad apathy towards the fixed ranking of the established figures. I have been recently struck by Mary O'Donnell's article "Suburban Blitz" in *Graph* which analyses the difficulties men have in relation to women's writing and some problems in women's attitudes to their own writing. I endorse one of her conclusions about "...inept reviewers and fainthearted publishers who at present lack the courage to publish new, intellectual and experimental writers of both genders...." As a sojourner in the land of the young-in-one-another's-arms across the Atlantic, the gravitas in Irish poem-making may seem over-glaring, but undoubtedly this middle to high "seriousness" rules the outlets. The lofty inability for the Irish media to take risks on the margins of poetry stems more from a lack of curiosity than a failure of nerve. As Ms. O'Donnell succinctly suggests the true pride of experience found in asking for hearts cannot be discovered in fishing for hearts of stone in Eastern Europe.

Though those who come back may pass through sailing-to-Byzantium expectation, thus imagining that the writing on the ground is airless, sullen, or "kitchen video", yet I make bold to offer some practical provocations. I am commenting now on writing in English and am not making a foray into the currently more holy sound of theory. The possibly plain fact to me is: Irish poetry needs informality. Its view of the poem is too tight, too line and stanza concentrated, too afraid of form and not afraid enough of content. It is peopled by influence and inhibition, not by ghosts or presences. No poet should be a hero to the audience or the media, as no gentleman was to his valet. Poems should not only be alive, the books that embody them should also be living. Construction of the book is not looked at in contemporary Ireland; the cover, typology, paging is conventional. Most books of poems look alike and give the dreadful impression it is enough to bring them out. They are slapped in front of the public. What is needed is a return, or recovery, to elegance and informality. If the production and reception of poetry is a community duty, then it is a bore. Magazines should offer different lines of development, special issues, quality debates. They must scream for more, they must beg for certain aesthetic considerations; one should be gender-free, another gender-loving. Some should always offer the goods quietly. There should be more journals (the country has excellent editors in the shadows); what publications there are should not print the same poets in roughly the same order at the same time of year for the same price. What would be innovative: the appearance of magazines that carried personal statements, diaries, logs of the imagination, exchanges of correspondence. Part of the legacy from the past of Irish poetry is prose such as Kavanagh's *Envoy* diary and Padraic Fallon's journal in *The Bell.* With further informality in writing and atmosphere, poetry could achieve special intimacies more than it does (though Thomas Kinsella strips his work to intimacy). I am thinking of the moment in the magical "Things Nobody Dies For" of Kavanagh; Carolan and Bridget Cruise stand in a field, they are alone as the voices representing sectarian violence fade, Carolan whispers, "I know you do not really mean what you say;/I know woman's nature ..." We could learn from Kavanagh's dialogue poems.

If poetry should be spoken as well as written, and it has become a script as much as a page, then it must be obvious that it requires a scene as music does. It may not be competitive but it aspires to the same condition. I am thinking of a series of rooms of varying space; when I was growing there were two "big houses" of apparently superior value: Clarke, Kavanagh and Fallon on one side, O Riordáin, Mhac an tSaoi, and Ó Direáin in the other field. There has to be a place; Bohemia is optional but for me it wasn't. Some autobiography will set up what I mean: there is a journey, even a going to the wars, in a younger writer's business. Literature was a rich foliage when I was on the look-out for it. It reads as luck when opportunity coincides with taste. I would not have liked to belong to Yeats' generation. Founding a country, elaborating a first consciousness, would not have been fun. How numbing to meet all the Olympians; I preferred what I got, all the Bohemians, a thing known before. I was pleased to have missed Pallas Athene in Ms. Gonne's straight back at Howth station. I was given Kavanagh's bent shoulders of the Cross, off Grafton Street.

A writer like me, coming back again and again as it were from the fairies, must face Irish poetries and possibilities honestly; my relationship with the society of poets cannot be entirely relevant or direct. There is dawn, noon, and sunset madness in art and they must not be confused. There is also the contrast of "pray for the wanderer" with the wonder of the parochial. A temptation is to use the modalities of one's odyssey to encapsule wisdom, and to dish it out relentlessly. One never knows the next few generations, and wisdom is the easiest thing they can do without. Perhaps also I am still too young to learn, as indeed some of the younger poets may not be. There is no duty to write poetry but there is one to strive for the objective. I may therefore serve *Poetry Ireland* magazine in particular (I had the honour of being on its editorial board in the sixties) by proffering some next to humble maxims, with the corollary that listening is not believing. May I try to sum up what I think I know about poetry on this blustery day of August, 1989; such contribution in part being based on the journey from McDaid's to everywhere and nowhere.

What are the Lucky Things for That Kind of Animal Soul We Used to Call The Poet:

I To live in the country, away from the lilacs and daffodils in city vases.

II But not to forget: if you are sitting in the same pub during the holy hour with writers like Kavanagh, Behan, Ó Nualláin (not to leave out the distinguished visitors like Theodore Roethke, John Berryman, etc.) you realise you are sitting in the Roman Empire or the 18th century; a single pillar in McDaid's marked the lounge.

III After a great generation or two (if you bring in the drawingroomers) a reaction to be looked at includes, obscure thyself in some habitat of exile. That exile must be full of the sound of broken glass: punning.

IV After seeing so many laurelled brows one must walk hatless in the rain, for half a mile.

V The dandruff of destiny must fall on the words in your clothes.

VI You are the poet; no I am not the poet; yes yes you are the poet; no no I am not the poet. What are you having?

VII One must dine in unimportant places where there are few restaurants.

VIII Literature is tips.

IX This is a quotation from Andre Gide, "Life in the eternity of the moment ... *nunc, in tempore hoc* (Mark, 10:29)
even now.
... et *nunc est* (John 4:23; 5:25)."

This is the moment to depart. There inspire to song nine muses.

Poetry Ireland Review (1989)

"A SUP OF THE HAWK'S, OR THE SAINTS": BECKETT AND IRISH THEATRE

As a child I was hypnotized by a line of Thomas Davis so redolent of our private despairs churned into public, historical calamity, the line about "From Dunkirk to Belgrade" lie the officers and soldiers of the Irish Brigade. As adults then, some of us crossed over into modernism, and now we have our soldiers scattered in the earth of European capitals: Joyce in the Fluntern at Zurich and Samuel Beckett in Montparnasse. In a book about Switzerland, by the Wisconsin writer Herbert Kubly, I am quoted as remarking about Joyce's grave, which, as many readers may remember, portrays a studious man reading a book; I observed that "a bottle and a glass would be more appropriate." I cannot imagine Beckett's resting place, but I know that the symbolic, historical writing of the Abbey dramatic tradition both leads into him and proceeds from him. That small but great stage was where much of twentieth-century Irish literature was fought for or over, indulged in, or spat out.

We knew a great playwright when we came to town in the 1950s. In Alan Simpson and Carolyn Swift's Pike Theatre, down an alluring lane, we saw a modern "miracle play." The following is how the poet Patrick Kavanagh saw that first Irish production of *Waiting for Godot*: "Part of this play's importance is that it both holds a mirror up to life and keeps reminding you, if you are interested in sincerity, that the reason you couldn't endure the theatre hitherto was that it was tenth rate escapism, not your dish at all." Now there was somewhere to go in the evening in addition to the pub. Apart from where it stands in world literature, *Godot* trumpeted a new phase of Irish theatre.

We knew that the tree in *Godot* was the tree of Yeats's *Purgatory,* the tree that had been fat, "greasy," with life and is now lifeless except for an illusion of illumination. The quotation from Beckett that is the title of this essay, written during the 1950s by him to the actor Cyril Cusack, comes as no surprise. We saw an Anglo-Irish tree of life reduced to its roots, to its idea; this minimalism was of the essence of the literary connection between them – as if Beckett were Yeats without the supernaturalism, and Yeats were Beckett without the realism. It seems to me that the plays of Yeats are assimilated to the core of Irish theater in the same ways as Beckett's; they are present and within the possibilities of the Irish drama of the 1960s and thereafter, but this joint influence is not up front or immediately visible. Their major contribution to contemporary Dublin theater is most obviously poetry: specialized emotional language, repeated extension of the image, and an elaborate naming of catastrophe. Yeats, of course, inclines to aristocratic relations, while Beckett endures human relations.

I cannot agree with Professor Nicholas Grene that the consciousness of Beckett in recent Irish playwrights constitutes an "uneasy awareness." My sense is that phrase should read something like "intense familiarity," a condition that could give rise to uneasiness. James Stephens described Yeats's plays as "masked" and "shrouded," terms that could refer to aspects of Beckett and also encapsule some of the thematic and technical developments in the work of Frank McGuinness and Brian Friel. Perhaps the historical and cultural subject demands such apparent obscurity.

I am sure Beckett used the common Hibernianism "sup" deliberately; apart from supping from the curing water of the Hawk's well, it would imply, in local code, desire and excess. In fact, Beckett must mean here's a "partaking" in some kind of magic substance, a belief that urges me to use another Celtic phrase, "second sight." I have wanted to apply this term for some time to Yeats, Beckett, Friel, McGuinness, and others such as Tom Murphy and Tom Kilroy. It suggests a kind of psychic overview of history, folklore, victimization (race and culture memory), pain, and the varieties of a syntax and rhythm not found elsewhere in English. Some will not see Beckett in this line, but I think a "native" edge can be detected in him, a resonance, a far seeing, hearing, and listening that come from having lived in Dublin, or Ireland, and having used that living aesthetically. Indeed, I discern a great postcolonial gift here: Beckett as the second patron of a great missed inheritance, an articulate voice speaking out of both sides of its mouth (Gaelic and Anglo). I refer to a condition of mind and speech that rejects both parochialism and provincialism, something priceless for the younger generations of dramatists. I am suggesting voice(s) that modify, enrich, and distance the Catholic tribal cultus that Friel and the younger dramatists have been deconstructing and remaking.

Beckett's contribution can be framed in Thomas Kilroy's terms: "The world of the Beckett plays is pre-social, pre-tribal, pre-communal, but one might as easily describe it as post-social, post-tribal, post-communal." I think Kilroy has, *inter alia,* the local context in mind. Beckett's closeness to the Irish tribe must arise primarily from participation as a young man in the Abbey's romantic rituals of Irishness; it is well attested critically that the closest Beckett gets to this in his texts are the homeless wanderers of Synge's *art nouveau* countryside. Beckett is the most private of Irish-born writers, a quality that led to his elaborations of silence on the stage. This dimming of exuberance is balanced by the singing and joking of his characters. It is noteworthy that Beckett eschews dancing, including Yeats's Salome-like "Noh," a tradition Friel restores with a vengeance in *Dancing at Lughnasa.* Friel, the next dramatist of importance after Beckett, and the father of the Young Turks of the 1980s, got what Yeats developed: salutory seasons of recuperating and retheorizing and a post-master's stage, in part divergent from Beckett, but related to him. Donegal has depths of the mind different from Dublin's. *Godot* and the other plays of Beckett's great middle period mushroom into moments in the later playwrights and sometimes become their stage devices and verbal ticks. While McGuinness and Friel adopt varying strategies, their sense of theatrical artifice primarily descends from Beckett.

This younger generation has perhaps the perverse luck of possessing political and cultural subjects that Beckett missed seemingly as a matter of chance; thus their connection with the older writer is conveniently veiled. Yeats had the "phantasmagoria" of 1916 and the subsequent Anglo-Irish conflict with which to work; Friel, McGuinness, and others are presented with the long-running Northern Ireland "troubles" to confront.

Beckett seems minimal in this political context, but he expresses harrowing descriptions of personal crisis in "West British," genteel Foxrock. That wealthy suburb and the National Theatre in downtown Dublin could hold cosy hands. Beckett, though politically remote by comparison, partakes of cultural "native" Irish procedures: he coats his birth and neocolonial upbringing with techniques borrowed in part from Gaelic sources. In particular, one notes Beckett's use of sarcasm and parody, and his adherence to singing and quotation. Beckett and Friel have a common need for some sort of earnestness at the heart of their drama: they trim their craft to its finest point, and they both insist on being in control of the text and timing of plays in production. In a sense, the spontaneity of their writing leaves nothing to the spontaneous.

A summary of what I am saying might read as follows: The "before" relationship within the Irish Dramatic Movement of Synge and Yeats to Beckett can be paralleled by the later adoption of Beckett by the group associated with Friel. As Beckett added an extra isolated voice to Synge's original characters (Martin Doul in *The Well of the Saints* is a fearsome pre-Beckett presence), so Friel and the younger playwrights take from Beckett tactical silence, pauses in monologue and duet, and abrupt and rhetorical philosophical discourses. Thus the last great Anglo-Irish writer is delivered into the hands of that other island of folklore and nationalist politics, and closer to that fated island's soil ambivalence. Friel, in the final expansions of his creative career, leads his characters in a descent into the shades in a manner similar to Beckett's. The characters are evicted from their past and from familiar occasions. Molly in Friel's *Molly Sweeney* is an example. In her isolated consciousness, every shape becomes an apparition; any person Molly remembers must undergo a fragmentation dance in her mind. Sometimes the voices in the two dramatists' work collapse from incessant reminiscing. In the background of both these writers is apparent a core idea of necessary self-sacrifice, some sort of breakdown of the hero's survival. This is another indication that Beckett did not get his "sup" from his Church-of-Ireland family who had no holy wells, no monastic saints, and no priest's jug of whiskey. There, the idea of self-sacrifice was not the paradigm of collective action.

Recent Irish drama abounds in Beckettian epiphanies, especially in devising a series of silence adjacent to an important or complete statement. Friel's handling of this approach sometimes includes "the speech from the dock." The best-known illustration of this is in *The Freedom of the*

City, where Lilly, Skinner, and Michael speak to the audience as they exit to be shot. The verbalization, highlighted by silence, is not a technique confined to ideological drama; it is often a sign of closure. Perhaps *The Faith* Healer provides Friel's most absolute command of this device. The curtain speech, ending with "At long last I was renouncing chance" and the direction "Pause for about four seconds. Then quick black," is the last unraveling of the protagonist, Francis Harvey, as man, artist, and conman. Beckettian focus and dissolution are everywhere in these dramatists: McGuinness, for instance, in *Observe the Sons of Ulster Marching towards the Somme,* inserts such a pause and silence in Pyper's crammed monologue in act 1. A new Irish stage liturgy has materialized, and it hails from Beckett's repertoire. These instances can appear as "sanitized" Beckett or "poor man's" Beckett. Of Pyper, in his first appearance, one may be tempted to remark, "Krapp's son speaketh." Friel takes Beckett's thorny dissolutions over the line: the major personae in *Freedom of the City, Faith Healer,* and *Aristocrats* are dead at the onset of the action; in the older writer they remain on the verge, one and a half feet from the grave. Friel's recent master-piece, *Wonderful Tennessee,* a rich, appealing compilation of history, folk religion, apocalypse, apologetics, and music, incorporates Beckett's range of language and theatrical suggestions and asides. Entwined family and friends meet on a remote pier with the intention of making a turas (pilgrimage) to an island that is variously a saint's place, the home of people of enchantment (fairies), and a place of ritual murder.

The pivotal moment – and the pure Beckettian catharsis – occurs when the group waits all night for the boatman Carlin (intimations of Charon, but the name might also be McGodot) to ferry them over. It must be Friel's intention for the theatergoers to be seized by nostalgia, for the reference is unmistakable. The characters see the boatman's house in the distance, they see a possible light in it, and of course Carlin never comes. The people on the pier sing, "Beyond the sand dunes / You will find the boat" (incidentally from "Abide with Me," one of Beckett's hymns). And so it goes on here and in later parts of the play. This question and answer, this hope and dismal echo, both reject and reanswer the small pandemonium and the endless vistas of locations already known in the theatre. In short, Synge's descendants are partying again, and their resolutions are just as wild and impossible.

David Richards, in his review of McGuinness's *Someone Who'll Watch over Me* in *The New York Times,* grasps the Beckett analogies: "Stripped of its political underpinnings [the play] calls instantly to mind the work of another Irish playwright, Samuel Beckett, equally preoccupied with waiting rituals in bleak places ... For no reason they can fathom, three people have been incarcerated, possibly forever, by unseen captors who may be vengeful madmen or irrational children, but in either instance exercise power quixotically. As the Irishman notes, two words sum up their plight: 'ridiculous, ridiculous.'" McGuinness's plays, especially his innovatingly brilliant *Carthaginians,* echo, mime, and even copy Beckett (with gales of Wildean wit added). The characters in *Carthaginians,* in particular the males, search for transformation, or change for change's sake, in their impossible habitations. They are Vladimir and Estragon as new Carthaginians waiting to be saved from Rome (England); in addition, Dido, the transsexual main role, magnifies the routines until he/she becomes a Godot older than Godot. The cemetery in the play is as claustrophobic as the room at the end of the world in *Endgame,* and here the resemblance is how McGuinness's characters rack each other with impossible and poetic demands. They are, in their pairings, Ham and Clov, an alternative community in an apocalyptic glow. As in Beckett, definitions become increasingly uncertain as they grow extreme and beautiful. The homoerotic tone of some Beckett stage characters is often renewed in these scripts. As Anthony Roche notes, in his *Contemporary Irish Drama: From Beckett to McGuinness,* many more more explicit passages can be read including, in *Observe the Sons of Ulster Marching Towards the Somme,* the line "I keep hearing the Dead." Roche points out convincingly that this is an echo of the refrain between Didi and Gogo ("Like all the dead voices").

These cross-currents are common to the aprés-Beckett Irish theater. In *Carthaginians,* McGuinness offers a play within a play, which becomes a comic and grueling satire on the gods of this theater: Yeats, O'Casey, Behan, and others. Despite all the borrowings, never a verbal hand is laid on Samuel Beckett. He is our perfect knight of the stage. He is in the text but not of the text. He is the Irish theater but not of it. He is us, not one of us. I call on Yeats to add the last word to this small celebration of influence: "the heart of a phantom is beating."

Essays in Honour of Melvin J. Friedman (2000)

Esau, My Kingdom for a Drink

– In asking you to remember those two noble kinsmen nuncle Riche and nuncle Edmund, Stephen answered, I feel I am asking too much perhaps. A brother is as easily forgotten as an umbrella.

Lapwing.

Where is your brother? Apothecaries' hall. My whetstone. Him, then Cranly, Mulligan: now these. Speech, speech. But act. Act, speech. They try to mock you. Act. Be acted on.

Lapwing.

I am tired of my voice, the voice of Esau. My kingdom for a drink.

You, James Augustine Joyce, of great and immeasurable constancy of soul, sailing between the Scylla of musty Protestant Ireland, Lyster, Best, Eglington, and the Charybdis of the neighbourly jealousy of your compatriot, Buck Mulligan, how much you speak for us. You, the greatest son of Catholic Ireland in seven hundred years, how many things you were to us, how near from our bogland you flew to the sun of truth of life, how like all of us you were searching for the father, Bloom-Shakespeare, hidden in the deep bones to which we long to return. How from the strangled city of the dead you carried your books as testimony of life, how from the decaying streets of your childhood you travelled with your poems, lonely Dubliner, to the sun, to your old father.

But above all you were speaking of the life which comes from the mind. You speak of the thoughts of house and father and mother and playmates on the road, then the years of learning your own body and looking and touching the bodies of others to find out that the thoughts of the mind are related to the touchings of the body, then the discovery – Flight No. I of the artist – that the mind works for itself, can see by itself, can understand beyond what it sees. And the recognition that the feelings of pleasure of the body are even deeper in the mind, that what you like in the body turns to what you love in the mind.

Your kingdom of the lonely tower of desire at sixteen. The paradise of desire at eighteen ripening into the earthlight of the hours and flowing with you to the bright faces at parties and pushing you even as far as the pubs. Then the going to college and the finding the world you were brought up for is a farce, that the professors you hear discussed are crooks or at best nonentities, that the priests surrounding you do not love their neighbour neither do they meditate but they worry about what effect they are having and what the Archbishop is thinking of their activities and how secure is the job and how long to go to a Parish. Where your mind awakens to reality, to the reality of your life now, and to the love which demands at the same time both angelic sublimation and the human tenderness of lusting. This was your smithy as well as mine, the young Dublin air, in which the mind trembles at last to art: the true craft of psychological man, the images of his dreams, of his ties to the earth of his birth. All that talking down the Dublin streets out of which our art begins: art by which you expressed your time and place and opened for us the closed doors of our destiny.

You Stephen-Daedalus, preparing in those streets to be an artist of all kinds and for all times, from the cry of your youth against the mob of College gombeens and censors to your end as the apotheosis of the artist as divine figure, the ultimate artificer of the deepest strands of holy life: myth and the dream. The Wake Man of civilization worshipped now where two or three are gathered in your name whether in New York or in the mid-West or at Santa Barbara, California. You are not a sick cult, as is still whispered in your town, but the cultus of the divine figure of the artist-doctor, the doctor who is his own guinea pig observing his own symptoms with the trained patience of a lifetime, and not only his life but everyone talking, laughing, suffering around him: society his national health list out of which he can only save a few, those who listen to his rhythms, look at his pictures, moralize his messages and endure the parable of his famine, the eaten-out heart of one man in one place.

You, James Joyce, artist-doctor with a few as the lucky heirs of your diagnosis, fierce old man of the Paris cafes, toiling over your prescriptions and all the time your patient dying under the microscope, silent warrior cold in the contempt of the shibboleths of your land, fatherpolitics and motherchurch across the narrow sea. You saw the water from the shore, greenbedabbled, and went on cleaning your weapons to scatter for ever the parishes of fat boozey men and crumbling anaemic women, your enemies. You made them all begin to die with Blazes Boylan, Mr. Deasy, Buck Mulligan, Fr. Conmee, the Citizen and all the shadows of the devil-soul of Ireland: you put them into your book and they became satirical caricatures and witches of hate. So you, James Joyce, loving us seriously all the time behind our backs like a father, caring for us as unmarried virgins who might die without kissing life, still walking our pavements from your books and showing us our hypocrisy and timeserving, comradeless, hoping as you wrote but telling none that we, in our green isle of only human snakes, should read your armoury of words and begin to live.

In the library you, Stephen-Joyce, talk about the stupid soul of the nation, of the bum scholarship and bogus renaissance of your fledging time. With the dead musty Protestant soul of Ireland, Lyster and Eglington, behind the counter whispering in the scared tones of Saintsbury and Dowden and beside you the shifty soul of townland Catholic Ireland, Buck Mulligan, with its student blasphemies and its pretense of classical education: that wild Ireland which settles down into the professions and makes money and gets bitter when it thinks of its youth and drinks and drinks. You in that library, with all Ireland wrapped around you in phoneyness and lies, and you setting them on the wrong track and making them think you were talking of Shakespeare and Ann Hathaway and whether he was the prince or the ghost but you were flying away, freeing yourself and laughing at them. And laughing most of all at Buck Mulligan the man with the knife between the smiles of his teeth, the mocker you drowned in mockery, the bawdy man you made dirt of until he was forced to turn respectable and call you an obsessive maniac but whose articles in American magazines attacking you had footnotes identifying him as a character in *Ulysses*. And Best the dusty celibate sleeping with the ideas of his books: something light in the style of Wilde he proposed to your wide soul, genes and genes away from that idiot pansy, the big man of putty who called small boys flowers and caressed them most unwittily, who tried to deflower they who are not flowerlike and who can not be plucked.

Genes and genes away from that you were in worship of the smiling face of the earth, the body of the woman offered and accepted by the clay of your sweet humble body, away from it in the love of your old father who looked in the bottom of his glass for your face and on the page of your genius for the promise that you would come back and talk to him, and away in the young man you were searching for the friend who would love your secrets and become your other self and cry with you and be about you and protect you, the friend who would hold you back from being shovelled in a coffin, as Paddy Dignam was, into an earth stinking with Glasnevin corpses, the friend who would tell you his love between the pub and the brothel and would become your angel and marry the other angel your woman waiting for you in the future, your woman who was of the salt of the sea and of the smell of Aran anemones, who became a Princess at your sight in Nassau Street, Nora your bride, the greatest Queen Ireland has ever had, a shining beauty of a woman whom you toasted in a million glasses: Princess, Queen, of the green slagheaps of Ireland and a greater one than Kitty O'Shea or Maud Gonne.

Your beautiful dream which I tell of in tears weeping over your Odyssey-truth: you listening to the earth, your ear deciphering the medley of sounds beneath the fields and towns, and smiling up at your wife and your friend, walking at dusk the streets of Dublin and looking for your wife and your friend. Your beautiful dream, Joyce, and of the provisions you took for the voyage and your face so peaceful in the storm and your struggle on and on, keening your father and your mother over the rough waves, and always in sight of the promised shelter where you would alight into the arms of your wife and friend. You made your voyage, Irishman, in sight of the ancestral angels whitening on the far shore uttering strange cries you tried to understand before you went asleep. Young hero, in the light of your chivalrous integrity, you travelled all, the mocking, the driving out, the sun, the sea, the waste, until you came for your evening meal to the house of the angels where your smiling wife and your friend were waiting for you.

And you, Stephen-James Daedalus-Joyce, among the books and the pale faces, sympathetic alien from the persecuted faith of your ancestors, David of the individual thinker against the priests and monopolists of Christ whose religion is the safety of their books and pulpits, clear thinker, descendant of Erugena, with a hunger for a Platonic absolute compatible with art, using the formulations of the Schoolmen to construct an aesthetic of the word, not the Word made Flesh, but the word made beautiful, the epiphany of the soul, whether of a girl on a strand or the Ballast Office clock the showing forth of the unutterable. You, secret Platonic heretic of the mysteries, pecking on the clever bones of Aristotle and Aquinas to parody the jerry-built mansion Ecclesia has made, you throwing their syllogisms back in their face speaking with your cruel irony of "the intellect" and "species" but yet wistful for the approval of the old bulldog of Aquino: respectful to the end of the system we are tombed and wombed in.

But above all you speak of the dissolving universe, the rain on the earth, the river into the sea, the flowing into the ocean, the vision of the soul early in the morning waking and dreaming and talking to itself in the cold light, before clothes are put on, shaving done and the world made everyday for safety: when you tremble near the shivering light in your blue bones: the lights with their heads of gods, the clouds in shapes of women, the fish carved from jewels, and the voice from the recess of your belly telling you to worship. You annotated them and made them into the substance of your all suffering craft, nearer the sun, hawker, you wrote them down, you read the writings on the wall of Heaven which sound mad to educateddull ears. You fled the nets of sense and learnt the rhythm of the tongues of God, the sources of language, the dialects of the tribes of Heaven you heard in the distance and you wrote the few you could translate down, fabulous penman. You, James-Joyce, holy word-giver of life.

More than any you chose life. You endured the stages of growing up, finding out how men live, and guarding yourself against your native vice, bitterness. Mostly you were hurt, human of the human, the insult received and the friend not at home, hurt in your longing for Ireland and her freedom and her ancient example, hurt in the family you had to look after, in the woman whose body you filled with flowers but whose tender flower could not see the light made from the beginning for her through her father, O family man whose odyssey was of the routines of meals and arrangements to catch trains, who wrote letters every night in your sleep to your old father and your aunt near Sandymount.

And the search for your friend, the comrade of your thought, your age, who is of Ireland, you speak of him everywhere in every page you search for the equal of your soul, the masculine of gender with an equal love. You in that library, in the European situation, the dialectic of Plato and Aristotle, crying with terrible bitterness; over your lost friend of your youth, he of Tinahely who left you whom you liked the best. How they all leave you alone on the strand or on the street, how he went from you, how being Irish they all leave you: to be alone, to go abroad with some woman, to be forgotten and damned. How the jackals of college watched their chances to get into the professions, how the jackals of the pubs watched the openings for their jokes, how the educated jackals, the scarecrows of the library, watched their reputations and their magazines and not you: you, lonely truth-sayer, with no comrade to tell it to, no friend to speak your heart to.

Only your father-friend, St. Leopold Bloom of everyman and every woman, is near you, waits for you, crosses you coming from the library, the knight of faith, of compassion of the blossoming earth: he lowers his eyes passing you, the light on the stone, as his heart beats for yours. And you know, you reach out, you a man with his work now cast: to put down everything that was there, what they said to you, what they did to you, what they are. And the one just man, St. Leopold Bloom of the blossoming earth, saves the city from the wrath of your gods, from the matches of your pen, the man who knew no distinctions, St. Leopold Bloom, who forgave everyone in the forgiveness of himself. The outcast, the Jew, the nobody Christ whom the citizens sneered at, waits for you, crossing you on the steps and mocked by Buck Mulligan, waits for you to take you to his house, his wife, his possessions, caring in the dead city of smear-souls to give you his skill at being ordinary, at being extraordinary, at being everyone: man O wondrous! woman O beautiful! earth how blossoming! You Jim Joyce, but a few hours away from your father's voice, from the kitchen of the artist-God, the Maker of words, the Delineator of analogies, binding your soul fast to your father on earth at 2 A.M. in Eccles St.

Now away from the quiet voices of the castrati in libraries, from the stuffed heads of patriots, you have money for a pint of stout, away from them, they have sold everything, their minds, their manhood, their land. You have been forgotten, Daedalus-Esau, acted on, made to salute them in the street, made to sign their documents, away from looking among them for friends, from thinking you can find a brother among them there is nothing here: You are the cheated Esau and your birthright has been taken from you and they have given you enough to buy a pint. Away, away.

You, James Joyce, lonely to-night in Zurich listening to the roar of the lions and hoping perhaps for the sound of children in boats off Killiney strand or for the calls of seagulls around the head of Howth in the early morning. Down in the town we have been celebrating you long: Up comes Tom McGreevy and he takes me by the hand. Let you and my boy join in the decent Joycean band.

The Gotham Book Mart (1962) / *The Abiko Quarterly* (1995)

THE FIGURE OF CHRIST IN D. H. LAWRENCE AND EDWIN MUIR

At this critical time in the conflict between the systems of East and West it is important to remember what decisively distinguishes the two ways of life. What we oppose, or what we should oppose, to the totality of State and work is an ideology of love and respect for the individual. Most of us, in the Christianized traditions of Europe, learn this ideology of love as much from the reading and expounding of the Gospel narratives as from the example of our parents. The events in the life of Christ, the miracles, the parables, become vividly familiar, and the replies of Christ to his questioners possess a poetic cadence that we hear in our ears for the rest of our life. There is one scene in particular which always remains at the back of our minds; a picture of such psychological power that it generates images of fear sufficient to overwhelm the conscious control of the mind. It is always the same picture, a darkened earth, soldiers standing about and a Man's agony crying from a cross:

> Whose is this horrifying face,
> This putrid flesh, discoloured, flayed,
> Eaten by flies, scorned by the sun?
> Whose are those hollow red-filmed eyes
> And thorn-spiked head and spear-struck side?
> Behold the Man: he is Man's Son.

The Crucifixion represents a primordial scene of guilt in our unconscious mind. It is a "symbol" in Jung's definition of the term: an action or word which signifies something relatively unknown in itself but known to be present by its dynamic effect. Thus the Crucifixion in David Gascoyne's poem is an example of the traditional psychological character of the suffering Redemption of mankind which finds its most striking and appropriate representation in the Cross. A cross in itself would have no transcendental association were it not for the symbolic interpretation projected on it from our childhood.

The figure of Christ, the prophet, the High Priest, has dominated the cultural thought of Europe as the most expressive ideal of the wise man, the holy man who teaches, the seer. In the vocabulary of Jungian psychology, the four Gospel narratives are the archetypal myths basic to the conscious and unconscious thinking of those people who over a long period of time have lived within the confines of a particular culture. Europe was an insular continent until the development of modern communications, and the themes, with their accompanying details, of the Gospels became the dominating system of symbols to explain man's profoundest hopes and fears in a universe which science had not yet penetrated. From the point of view of literary criticism, these archetypes are important because they share a disposition to produce over and over again the same or similar mythical conceptions. Thus the same stories, the same unexplained actions which have a traditional symbolic construction, the same type of hero-casting, occur in the great literatures of Europe. Erich Neumann has described the common, age-old groups of representational devices and hero figures in a particular culture as a cultural canon; a body of definite symbols which the people in a culture adopt as a collective expression of their Society.[1] Thus the art of Christian

Europe forms a distinct cultural canon, and this article illustrates what happens to the symbols of a canon when the culture of the civilization, which produced the canon, is breaking up. I have chosen the contemporary work of D.H. Lawrence and Edwin Muir to show what forms the response to a dying cultural canon can produce.

I say a dying cultural canon because both Lawrence and Muir lived outside a particular religious faith and had no explicit attachment to Christian dogma or theology. Of course, for writers who have such attachments, and there are many in Western Europe, the Christian canon is not dying but merely needs re-interpretation from the imaginative resources of each generation. But Lawrence and Muir wanted to change the classified Christian symbols of their predecessors from having a fixed evaluation to being at the disposal of the individual writer for his own purposes. They wanted the writer to exercise his own complete control over these traditional symbols; their aim, I think, was quite deliberate: Lawrence and Muir were deeply attached to the redemptive role of Christ in the Gospels, which they had learned in their conventionally religious childhoods, and they felt themselves free to organize subjectively their early experience of the Gospels. They were not directly concerned with whether the events in the life of Christ were historically true; they considered the narratives of the life of Christ as mytho-poetic structures transmitted in the past through Christian liturgy, art and popular devotion but now realizable by writers in purely literary contexts.

They were not alone in this endeavor; for example, Rilke was able to construct, without direct reference to his religious beliefs, an aesthetic which relied heavily on Christ, Our Lady, and the angels. Perhaps the nearest analogy is the attempt by Van Gogh to produce paintings which would be Christian and yet have traditional religious iconography: he looked on the forms of nature he painted as the sacramental visible sign of an inward spiritual grace. He once said: "I want to paint men and women with something of the eternal which the halo used to symbolize, and which we seek to convey by the actual radiance and vibration of our coloring." Van Gogh wanted to substitute for historical iconography, which is known to those brought up in the Christian canon but has to be learnt by those coming (increasingly) from outside it, an iconography of color and forms relations which revealed itself spontaneously to the onlooker: he expected the symbols of Christ and Gospels to be so deeply hidden in the unconscious that they could be transferred to a completely new dimension by art – that of light and color.[2]

John Middleton Murray has pointed out that D.H. Lawrence, from this point of view, was a deeply religious man whose whole life can be represented without distortion as a struggle with the Christian cultural canon as he understood and experienced it.[3] Lawrence disregarded the supernatural elements in the living Church; one aspect of his terrible tragedy was that his non-conformist religious training prevented him from having any contact with the Christian symbols as practiced in liturgy and Catholic devotions. Lawrence knew nothing of the Sacraments; nothing of the great images of the Church, Baptism, Absolution, Agape, the Eucharist, the Cross. He was ignorant, at least partly, that the psychic structures of such images reach back, beyond present practice and developed rites, to the roots of primitive religion in early Christianity. But he realized that the Christianity he knew had become institutionalized and he resisted the lukewarm Christ of modern Protestantism. The struggle is preserved in the introduction Lawrence wrote to the Grand Inquisitor section of the *Brothers Karamazov*; he felt that the figure of Christ as ethical ideal is inadequate and he adopts the Grand Inquisitor's criticism of Christ as loving men in the wrong way by placing on them the intolerable burden of unselfish love, in asking them to choose between "earthly and heavenly bread" and "to judge between good and evil."[4] Lawrence did not reject Jesus; he still regards Him as the great lover of mankind who expects too much of men.

In his later work Lawrence turns to the figure of Christ as the focal point of religious consciousness. A fictional attempt to deal with the problem is his story "The Man Who Died", with its theme of a crucified prophet who comes back from the dead not to continue preaching but to find reality in a woman, the priestess of Isis, who awaits the coming of the dead Osoris. Christ is equated with this physical consciousness, with which Lawrence positively identifies himself, and he saw the future religion as "a resurrection into touch." It is this "physical tenderness" which Lawrence comes to see as the authentic core of Christ's teaching, thus admitting that his new religion is derivative: an extension into consciously physical terms of the Gospel love of one another. The awareness of a possible resurrection of the flesh is the seminal image in the last phase of Lawrence's creativity; its fullest statement (if you bypass *Lady Chatterley's Lover*) is to be found in *Last Poems*. Paradoxically the awareness he was striving for brought him to a half reconciliation with the Catholic Church, at least its Latin form around the Mediterranean: "The Old Church knew best the enduring needs of man, beyond the spasmodic needs of to-day and yesterday … For centuries the mass of the people lived in the seasonal rhythm, under the Church, and it is down in the mass that the roots of religion are eternal. Whenever the mass of a people lose the religious rhythm, that people is dead, without hope. But Protestantism came and gave a great blow to the ritualistic and religious rhythm of the year, in human life." The religion of "touch" Lawrence knew lacked a background and he felt this might be given by his exotic version of Latin Catholicism. The idea receives a final utterance in the last thing Lawrence wrote, a deeply sympathetic review of Eric Gill's *Autobiography*. In it he blames the Church for having on the whole caught the malaise of the Protestant Churches in preaching an ethical Christ. He asserts the necessity of a living instinctive faith in God, different from the moral ideal of a "good" God.

D. H. Lawrence's ultimate position, I think, can be assessed as a personal attempt to revolutionize the contemporary Christian canon. His effort was an original manipulation of the central Symbol of the Christian Faith to give the "myth" a new imaginative life. I feel Lawrence considered the Church had failed to integrate the figure of Christ into a sacramental unity with physical life; he tried to add to the figure of Christ a new physical dimension. Lawrence wanted to make Christ a full representative physical man, leaving to one side his divinity, to make a new body as well as a new heaven and a new earth:

> To know a man as we have never known
> a man, as never yet a man was knowable, yet still shall be.

Edwin Muir's contribution is altogether different from that of Lawrence's. Muir was a less gifted writer in many respects than Lawrence but the former's interpretation of the symbols of the Christian canon is wider and profounder. What is there in Lawrence's imaginative experience to compare with the central vision of Muir's poetry: the images of the journey on "the great road of time"; Greeks returning from Troy; the centers of the Judeo-Christian cycle such as the Fall, the wanderings of Abraham and the Crucifixion and Resurrection of Christ; and Muir's own return to his folk childhood on the Orkneys? The imaginative range is wider; of man locked in the recurrent fable of history rather than an individual destroyed by the mechanistic conformity of an age.

Muir became a Christian late in life; the exact nature of his Christian beliefs is still obscure but his imagination was completely satisfied by the spiritual truths and poetry of the Gospels. Before that his poetry had been developing an inherently religious attitude. R. P. Blackmur has compared the feeling of reverence in Muir to Croce's description of the pietas of the *Aeneid*: "A human feeling of bitter memories, of shuddering horror, of melancholy, of homesickness, of tenderness, of a kind of childish pietas".[5] These qualities are all present in Muir but I would add to them the respect of holiness for the diversity and depth of each created thing: this quality is analogous to the "natural piety" of Wordsworth. Both poets perform the act of reverential belief in "the types and symbols of Eternity" existing in the organic world. The pietas of Muir drew him relentlessly to the images of the Christian tradition.

"Incarnation" is a keyword in the elucidation of Muir's poetry. Muir describes in his autobiography how the images of Incarnation enveloped him during his stay after the war in Rome as British Council Representative: "In Rome that image was to be seen everywhere, not only in churches, but on the walls of houses, at crossroads in the suburbs, in wayside shrines in the parks and in private rooms. I remember stopping one day for a long time to look at a little plaque on the wall of a house in the Via Degli Artisti, representing the Annunciation. An angel and young girl, their bodies inclined to one another, their knees bent as if overcome by love, tutte tremente, gazed upon each other like Dante's pair; and that representation of a love so intense that it could not reach further seemed the perfect earthly symbol of the loves that passes understanding".[6] The poems of Muir's late period, from *Journeys and Places* (1937), often take for their subject different events in the ministry of Christ. In "The Transfiguration" Muir imagines that at the moment of the Transfiguration everything was transfigured, mankind and animals, and even the simplest natural objects. "The Annunciation" is a direct transcription of the experience that Muir describes in his autobiography. One of the greatest of his poems with this feeling is "The Killing," canvass of the Crucifixion in which the intensely realized details give the impression of an actually remembered scene.

Muir approaches the incarnate archetype of Christ in another interesting way: he sets it in its historical order. He has written several soliloquy poems in Hellenic settings which prefigure the coming of Christ. The most significant of these poems is "Prometheus" where that mythological hero, chained for all time to a rock, dreams that, when the world ends, the gods may ask him to come back among them again. But Prometheus has heard a rumor that the gods live no more, that Someone greater has taken their place; he wonders whom he shall find:

At the world's end to whom shall I tell my story?
A god came down, they say, from another heaven
Not in rebellion but in pity and love,
Was born a son of Woman, lived and died,
And rose again with all the spoils of time
Back to his home, where they are now transmuted
Into bright toys and various frames of gold;
And Time itself is there a world of marvels.
If I could find that god, he would hear and answer me.

In this series, in addition to "Prometheus" there are "The Labyrinth", "Oedipus", "Soliloquy"; Greek necessity is reconciled with the transcendental freedom won on the "tormented wood" of the Cross. The Redemption is the completing image in the sequence: the controlling tension between Muir's dreaming and waking world. Christ as symbol of Grace is the living vehicle into which all mythologies pour, as likewise it is the dream in the intuition of immortality. The fundamental sources of Muir's creative insight were myth and dream: dream gave entrance into myth and myth into history fulfilled in fable; every individual was to him an immortal spirit destined to re-enact the whole life of man from the unconscious, extending beyond the Fall, to the Redemption of the conscious mind in Incarnation and Crucifixion. Muir responded absolutely to the significance of the symbols of the Christian canon; for him they sum up man's search for stability at the heart of mental flux. He is the only English writer of this century who, in his mature work, adhered exclusively to our dominant archetype.

Lawrence and Muir, the former in his fragmentary personal way and the latter in his total imagination, composed in the ambience of traditional Christian imagery. What advantage do they derive from so doing? Other, perhaps greater, writers, such as Joyce, Yeats and Pound worked outside the Christian Canon in older traditions. The answer perhaps suggests itself in the mental climate we inhabit in reading Joyce, Yeats, Pound: there is an atmosphere in their work which, despite its magnificence, is one of staggering isolation from the society around them. This sense of total isolation of the artist is, of course, most marked in Joyce and it is much less extreme in Pound who, at an unfortunate phase in his life, found his connection with the tragically uprooted society of our time. What we most miss in their work is the reconciling, distancing figure of Christ and we cannot find ultimate reassurance when the imaginative hope of the Gospel symbols is absent. The reader has to bypass his deepest images and relate the meaning of their books to esoteric symbols, the distorted world cycles evidenced in the eccentric puns of *Finnegans Wake,* the astral planes and cabbalism of *A Vision,* the ideographs and the tangled economics of *The Cantos.* In a sense the achievements of these great contemporary writers remain monuments of man's non-fulfillment in the leisurely life civilization has made for him. They can never be disregarded but their contact with their audience, outside the exclusive circles of universities, is fitful: they are ideologically divorced from the group, the community of responses. For the symbols chosen by artists, the true aristocrats of society, should be communicable as any public ritual or domestic celebration.

Art can only become public again, in the fullest sense, when its symbols, despite the multiple complexity of their subject matter, rise from the shared associations of the Christian mysteries. Thus Lawrence and Muir may be treated as forerunners; among the first who made their way with their words into the changed – more humanistic, more imaginatively earthy – numinosum which is the centre of our particular culture. In contrast to them T. S. Eliot has written out of the wasteland of that beleaguered Christian culture, unchanged by modern progress or philosophic thinking. T. S. Eliot belongs to the past, to the history of English literature which he has re-written to present its completion with his own work. Lawrence and Muir are not inside the classical traditions of Western Europe or historical Christianity as T. S. Eliot is; the former come to Christianity as the maximum material for understanding Western European man. And one solution for contemporary existential anguish, inherent not only in Sartre and Camus but also in Beat writers such as Allen Ginsberg and Norman Mailer, can be found in a religious context, in a participating assimilation of the traditional Christian symbols imaginatively exploited so as to explain to man the meaning of his fearful universe of pain. The Church, for doubtless sound historical reasons which a theologian could elicit, has not overtly encouraged in modern times humanistic realization of the figure of Christ. The Church's concern has been, in human terms, with the passions and deliverance from sin. This emphasis has led to the unfortunate notion that religious awareness is hostile to progress, including progress in the arts. A correction to this tendency would lie in a creative sharing by the modern writer of the religious symbols given to us by the Christian teaching of our childhood. At least in

Ireland this Christian teaching is the common early experience; to be neglected in our art at the expense of not communicating to an audience but instead of arousing hostility.

One cannot say, even in Ireland, that subjects with an implicit Christian symbolism should be the only subjects of art and poetry. The artist can work validly in any tradition he chooses as long as he relates it to his own experience: the poet can work in a different or indirectly related aesthetic; as Robert Graves has done in his cult of the White Goddesses; or he can present man without myth as Wallace Stevens has done. But in this country, for the writer with a Catholic background, the ultimate direction of his work is bound up with the attitude he takes to his religion. If he is to integrate himself with the sensitive needs of his people he must use, in part, the Christian material he shares with his neighbor in every townland. Otherwise, as now, the writer's world will tend to be private, admission on production of a university degree.

The University Review (1963)

NOTES

1 See his discussion in *The Eranos Year Books III*, 1958, pp. 3-37.

2 W. H. Auden comments on this aspect of Van Gogh in *Encounter*, Vol. xii, April, 1959, p. 40.

3 *The London Magazine*, May, 1956, p. 57.

4 *The Grand Inquisitor*, introduced by D. H. Lawrence, 1930, p. ii.

5 "Between the Tiger's Paws", Kenyon Review, Vol. XX, No. 3, Summer 1959, p. 420.

6 *An Autobiography* by Edwin Muir, 2nd Edition, London, 1954, p. 278.

NOTES ON THE WANDERING CELT: AIDAN HIGGINS' *BALCONY OF EUROPE*

> The Irish may be as common as whale-shit – excuse me – on the bottom of the ocean – forgive me – but they do have imagination.
>
> – Djuna Barnes, *Nightwood*

Aidan Higgins's 1972 novel *Balcony of Europe* is a stab at establishing a major work, on which the basis of a canon may grow. Thus it is self-consciously in harrying pursuit of Irish times past (also pastimes, if you understand the tribe). Two of the commonest criticisms fielded against Higgins have been his derivations in style and personal narrator mannerisms from Joyce and Proust; he has been regarded, justly in his early work, as a neo-Joycean, and in *Balcony of Europe* he has been accused of the airs and graces – to use native slang – of a "spoiled Proust." This novel attempts to create a structure, and aesthetic content, by ignoring such comments and by concentrating on the traditional concept of exile in a new form. The novel begins and ends with faded slices of internal emigration in Ireland, and between is sandwiched the expatriate slum of the Spanish coast in the sixties: the dreadful mass elitism of golden beaches whose comic vulgarities Higgins rips apart with Celtic thoroughness. Here the narrator-painter preens himself, observes various rootless types, and takes in prose and alcohol in rhythmic patterns. The faults of the alien exile society are faultlessly bestowed in the eye of the beholder.

A problem in the novel is undoubtedly airs and graces, both of poetic prose purple sketching and of the protagonist's upper-echelon tone. The question of class must remain. Firstly, the work is novel-autobiography down to some characters known personally to me, and secondly it is the traditional defense of the artist, something on the lines of my coldness, my rudeness, my calumnies do not matter because in art I am recreating my society and its temporal climate. Higgins in his alter ego, Dan Ruttle – a somewhat facile Symbolist transference from one art form to a neighbouring one – is always a gentleman with memories of the lost house of paradise and with the bitter consolation of defeat and poverty for his parents. Stephen Dedalus, to his credit, is never a gentleman; Joyce's greatness partly rises from the fact that he never entangles his talents in the worst net of all, snobbery. In fact, Higgins dissects snobbery like Proust. His way around it is to metaphorize on a big canvas: Dublin, Sligo, to convey decay; the Aran Islands suggesting regenerative waters of life; the Costa Del Sol , in its tourist-village suburbs suggesting flotsam and jetsam. European past thrown overboard to lighten WW II pain. The large middle section of the work is taken up with this environment as a ship of fools: artistic American Jews, a Nazi baron from the Baltic, and an able exponent of the *vice anglais*. The Plaza, about which the bars of the café-ship of fools are set, is stage and deck. Finally, the Balcony of Europe is the name of Ruttle's favorite bar. The Celt finds his destiny in the usual place, a magic Cana watering hole.

This novel is both major and minor, both over-written and under-felt – both blemishes are, however, solid in the context. A vanity fair could not be put together without these qualities. It is, for example, too long – a pig of a book, to use another nativism – it might be a journal translated into a novel; a European fiction form in itself. Boorish with words yet planted with lovely prose poems of landscapes. Garish with jewelry yet hungry for more life than can be sustained; a tribute to the fed and the dead. And definitely a take-it-or-leave-it piece.

The style, so pure, cold, and long-suffering, needs a word of explanation. To veer away from the masters, Joyce and Proust, Higgins takes stylistic rides into the territory of lesser yet immortal folk. Flashes of *Nightwood* occur in both dramatic monologue and in character. Both the Baron (even to title) and the English angel of "How strange the home-fire!" are recreated from Djuna Barnes' work. For surface, he parades tidbits from Durrell's *Alexandria Quarter*, down to the name of the narrator's wife Olivia and to back pages of work notes in the form of rejected epigraphs. If a major theme is the stealing of pieces of other couples' wedding cakes, Higgins ices them perfectly. In the background of his rhythms, digressions, and monstrous flashbacks I hear the cloying echo of the garrulity of the most minor of Irish masters, George Moore. The feeling in Higgins is that there is nothing that an extended anecdote can't do to improve a book. Do as Moore did when stuck with dictating to his secretary: pile on the memory and fish out a story from the sea of narcissistic reflections. In *Balcony of Europe,* though, this habit is as revealing as [it is] irritating. The book matches the restlessness of the reader, in a way *Hail and Farewell* cannot.

A lot of the action takes place on beaches and swimming near them. The Celt seeks the warm golden places to find the temple of love, like any northern European. This book takes the shape of a ritual invocation of Venus rising from the sea. It closes with a love-swim which refers back to the adulterous water-plunging with Charlotte, the fatal American siren to the painter's erotic self-preoccupations.

The book is Shakespeare's "Two Loves I Have." One given by the early plot, the other rendered up by the beach and the waves. It is the culture of ladies, of the Lady:

> From his position he must have had a good view of Venus in the sea, flutter-kicking along, her posteriors rolling like porpoises. *El sol rompío su envoltura , las mujeres se miraban asustadas.* O, lady, when the sea caressed you, you were a marble of foam. He called out a greeting in Gaelic, invoking the mother of God. (446)

The material is largely familiar to Irish readers. The early sketches of the old age and decay of the father and mother are parallel in location and type, even to a detail like anti-Semitism, with the situation in Hugh Leonard's *Da*. The difference is stylistic and in terms of social class. The fall of man, the fall of the narrator's house, parodies the fall of Ireland, both Celtic and Anglo-Irish, to the seediness of itself in a peasant state, to the contemporary country with the upstart Tiberius ruling on an island. Like all good literature out of this super-bog, the result is a new tour of the nuances of Irish history. It is like, once again, life in a ruined castle. An example would be: who but an Irish reader, or an American Joyce scholar, would see the point and absorb the luxury of the reference when Higgins ends a purple prose-poem short section, fantasizing the fucking of Charlotte with a male friend, with "Oh Queenie!" The woeful, wonderful entrance of Parnell's Kitty O'Shea and Ireland mythopoetic love-bed. Another curiosity of the book is the continual presentation of Brendan Behan as a man of homo-fire, as the corrupt Caesar, the Dublin gutty, and the impotent lover. Behan is dragged through the mud – some of it his own, it might be admitted – as a sort of base relief to the narrator-author's sorrow post-and-ante-coitus. There is a sort of camp-macho ingredient in Higgins' writing which can be left to the reader's taste. On the other hand, I would prefer a life presented in art that wouldn't be any harsher but would contain, somehow, more sweat.

Towards the end of the work the narrator confesses, "Yes, I like backward countries." Yes, I like them too. They disappear so fast we have to write about them.

The Review of Contemporary Fiction (1983)

WORKS CITED

Barnes, Djuna. *Nightwood*. London: Faber and Faber, 1936.

Durell, Lawrence. The *Alexandria Quartet*. London, Faber and Faber, 1968.

Higgins, Aidan. *Balcony of Europe*. London: Calder, 1972.

Moore, George. *Hail and Farewell*. Washington, D.C.: Catholic University Press, 1985.

WITH MICHAEL HARTNETT IN SPAIN AND MOROCCO 1964

The "T" had not yet come into his name; there was still an unbardic non-native echo to it. National authenticity had not quite been defined; the countryman was there but the countryman in the city had not consolidated. There was now a turning to the Mediterranean, to the gods and goddesses of its amphitheaters and dry walk-arounds, the wine and garlic lanes, and across the British-monkey-watched sea to the fez and turban in twentieth century glitter and French Deco spas (just being vacated). A gorgeous curtain was going up on new Bohemian artmaking, twisting in the Beat music from the clubs of the United States, and we wanted to balance it with a Graeco-Roman basis. Then Michael could return to the McDaid's promenade and rest areas of Co. Limerick, and I to the similar swan-singing around Kavanagh and convalescences of Co. Wexford.

Michael, Barry Cusack and I arrived in Malaga airport and shortly afterwards found ourselves in a basement bodega with young white-aproned guardians of the wine. Each order was on the slate, and at the end of a stretched evening we offered to pay but none knew the amount. A gracious introduction to the land of Francisco Franco, Lorca's singing ghost, and Philip II's gout-chair. Next morning a tram to the beach but we had no time to contemplate a swim: a row of bar-restaurants knelt invitingly on the sand with fresh fish cooking. Talking is a reflection of landscape and we were instantly lyrical, Barry drooping behind us. Next morning we were in La Linea; up on the roof of our hotel we saw and knew the Moorish world with the crickets' sound. So Lorca was in the continuing line of these ghosts.

I got a swim on the beach next to the rock of Gibraltar, Michael guarding the heap of my possessions; we leant away from the monkeys and did not cross over into that portion of empire. We went instead to the ferry and saw the blue hills of Africa looming up. Michael started talking about Hemingway. Our guide kidnapped us on landing though we had the name of a French hotel in the casbah. At the registration desk Americans were asking where Paul Bowles lived. Sitting in the Socco Chico, interzone passed in its charming and furtive costumes. I made us go to the French section to look for Tennessee Williams. In the morning, Ahmed was in our bedroom patiently waiting for his gentlemen to wake up and moan their hangovers. He told us about girls and boys; the latter cost twice as much because it was not as right. Michael asked him about keif; that was not good either. He took us to the party of our lives on Tangier beach. All night at one end we kept sending for beer as three musketeers entertained us; they seemed to live in a space under the sand. They said they were in Franco's Foreign Legion. They saluted the Spanish flag with a fascist hymn: our face to the sun. Their concluding act was to go down their hole, then come up in women's clothes and wiggle for us. The next night we went to a club and young Arab girls danced; at least, Barry and Michael thought they were girls.

We headed for Xauen up in the mountains; James Crosbie had told us about it in McDaid's. Michael must have got some keif somewhere; our bus was stopped by the police, and Michael in agitation let some fall. It spilled across the floor but the officials were not interested in tourists. We put up in a Berber hotel and explored. I walked up the hills and lay down under an ilex tree. Camels passed. Michael went wandering to the new hotel on the town's edge and spied a car with Irish number plates; he was revolted. The Spanish had just left. Spaniards were running empty cafes. We bought drinks for youngsters because they were not bound by the Koran. They said their families had keys to houses in Granada. Back in the hotel room, Michael read Neruda.

We were discovering Morocco was more expensive than Spain so back on the ferry. Lovely fish soup brought by old Algeciras waiters. Return to the caverns of Andalucia. We were becoming culture trained, alternating beer and wine, soup with bocadillos; Lorca began his possession of us. I was hooked on his images of sexuality and death; Michael took his rhythms and syntax as the later poems sometimes showed. I took his boy heart; Michael took his sailors and gypsies in their trapped adoration of female beauty. Michael loved the fantasies of Lorca's narration, particularly the long gaze of Narcissus into the pool. Michael became sort of a drowned man. I noticed another strange thing: the cityspaces, the snow-flirting hills of Andalucia seemed more insubstantial than Morocco. The three of us moved in them like exhausted spectres.

Our time to part our ways in a foreign "poetry junk yard" had come. We went to a corrida in Cordoba and wrote our temporary elegies for friendship by the throes of the bull. On the wall outside the Plaza de Toros, Michael and I took a quick wine-breath goodbye. He was going for a while to Madrid and Barry to Cadiz. Michael wrote a few times from Madrid He wanted to buy a house there for £50. As nobody believed you could buy a house in Spain for that amount – not even in Avila, John Jordan added – I accepted the McDaid consensus and did not remit the money.

Michael poured out his observation and passion for the exotics of Tangier, Tetuan, and Xauen in his "Persian

Sequence" (in Arena 3) "... had flowers genitalia/all women would be lesbian." Michael's more major work was reserved for Spain, its tortured history, its empire of slavery and Roman excess, its Madonna-lit violence, the lonely tabernacles of its writers. Michael had a crisis in his life; he recorded his painful love-past, his Catholic child-doom, his paranoia of the dispossessed ("Thirteen Poems Written in Madrid," in *Arena* 4). He came smack up against the twentieth century: "he is dying, the coin adorner/and he will be mourned,/for what are principles in face/of cheap wine, cheap cigarettes? On every wall and window/the king has writ these words: '25 años de PAZ'."

These are a few notes on a vatic adventure in the time before poets became a new kind of celebrity.

The Shop (2000)

I MUST BE TALKING ABOUT MRS. CALDWELL TO EL REY DE SON ARMADANS

I think it is right to say that Camilo José Cela was King of Palma de Mallorca when I lived there in the sixties. Circumstances may have changed since then; things do not stand still even for fiction writers who keep changing their forms and styles. Then Cela was the quasi-legitimate Regent (a slightly less vulgar word than King) in matters of *belles lettres* that are always important for Spaniards on an island where magic becomes tourists. In my memory, Cela was the definite belletristic beast on this luxury isle of Prospero, living above and around neighbors such as Miró, Edward Dahlberg the writer of *poems en prose*, Robert Graves the prose writer, and three translators extraordinary to the English language: Anthony Kerrigan, Alastair Reid and R. F. C. Hull. Cela gave a certain twilight, in the El Terreno district below the castle, to this activity; I could feel his mocking but not unromantic voice on certain terraces, a strange going-down-to-water feeling. It seemed it was he who played dark but not very dreamy bars in a singular reservation, where a husky and cruising version of Mrs. Caldwell's English language was spoken. He seemed to contribute the jolly ashen face of Batista, the Cuban dictator, walking along the seawall with pudgy doppelgangers – a placement for one of the colonels that Cela must have sweated under when he was a soldier for Christ and Spain. I suspected him, too, of following a gang of freckly Irish kids from Queens, and from the 6th fleet, along my street looking for a party. Everything on that island under the muse nose of Cela.

Here is a poem I wrote under this order:

El Fervor de Palma

On another evening, when it is not easy
To hold together a religio sensually overflowing,
What is so laden out there with yellow
It fans the dusk to honey?

An Alexandrian wind overheats
Though in December lemon trees,
And down flights of long steps
A coming of twilight vendors.

Cela embodies, over every other quality wherever he has lived or lives, Nietzsche's "aliveness." But, despite some early quaint verse, Cela is not a poet. He does not wish to make the world sacred, a theocracy of the seven veils or the seven churches. Cela, for all the shape-changing charisma, is the essential prose writer. He wants to embellish life. He often uses the tradition of the grotesque to desacralize; his comedy tends to be very black coffee. Sometimes he refrains from farce, without removing all its elements, and instead throws into the ring a work, like *Mrs. Caldwell Speaks to Her Son*, that carries an inheritance of feeling. This just-about-novel is both a modernist language plea and a gloating of pre-rhetorical eloquence. The work is the nearest Cela strikes to poetry without wounding it. The short chapters become like boxcars in a long winding Spanish train: in this sparkling art of sub parable, the author confronts the differently aroused expectations of his readers through diary, dreams, and dharmas; or a little realism, a little surrealism, and some spirit. The reader is sent back to his after-womb, to his thought process of imagination, and to his or her own distortion of ancestor worship. The reader is made to talk to his or her childhood, to some parent figure walking slowly to exit, sunset, Calvary. Cela puts into the voice of Mrs. Caldwell the space left by desertion.

Before I speak more about *Mrs. Caldwell Speaks to Her Son* (which was written long before Cela became the Gamecock under the Palma palm trees), perhaps I should explain what I was doing in Mallorca. For none of us is it a simple tale of a writer in exile: for me it had to do with the most terrifying phenomenon on earth – a mother's love for her child. I had to escape from the strategies of the womb to a less warm climate – though I had not to go as far as Eliacim "who was as tender as a maidenhair-fern leaf and who dies heroically in the tempestuous waters of the Aegean Sea." In Palma, *Mrs. Caldwell Speaks to Her Son* flew into my hands. I recognized at once that its subject matter was my problem and that its style was the construction of a great mannerist. And I was dazed by its continually honking 213 chapters: it was as if Ezra Pound had commanded, "Make it new and long."

Mrs. Caldwell Speaks to Her Son may be, as everyone confesses, a strange book, but it remains a mainstream classic on perhaps the most intimate theme in literature – the sexually tinged love a mother possesses for her son. The mother puts her son on a pedestal of memory and fantasy and prays for him, weeps for him, undresses for him. In chapter 42 she says, "The father, your father, my dear, was never more than a decorative element, the excuse for our being able to love, in the son, all his virtues: those which have form and those which don't; those which have a name and those which don't; those which serve for something, and those which, strange as it may seem, also serve for something." Mrs. Caldwell finally decides on her offering to Eliacim; she must die through madness in order to suffer for him and perish like him. The diary turns into an alluring pool of disjunction from reasons for living. She both expands and squeezes her imagination; she transforms herself and then disappears as we watch the wreckage of her heroism. "Nothing can destroy a mother's love": this cliché sums up the wisdom of generations. We hear the speech of David over Absalom: Mrs. Caldwell can be interpreted as biblically murmuring; this is my beloved son, in whom I am well shrouded. Death, this is my sting, a full, pleasant one.

This work could be made into a manual of son raising, especially only-son raising. It must be the *admonitum* against son worship. The tone of David crops up the whole time (and Absalom was not even an only son); "Yes, he's my son, my only son; his name is Eliacim." How wonderfully Mrs. Caldwell deals with the problem; she exorcises the pain of his loss by recreating him sexually: "Dance that tango with me, dear, press me close against you, and hum those repulsive words that give me back my youth and fill my heart with evil intentions." She is sweetly and stupidly British: "My son, unless you love tradition, you will not see luxuriant orchids, nor, rather white lilies, growing in your heart, the lilies that make useful reputations." The novel allows the author to indulge in charming addresses to himself as a young punk-writer, as in the chapter "The Bad Part Comes Later." The novel has many uncanny Richard Brautigan moments, an eerie Californian echo (an obvious example of cart before horse). There are exquisite old Castilian moments throughout: I like the hidalgo refrain about the lack of dignity in working. There congregate on certain pages Cela's mordant notes on the fall of the British Empire, as witness the remarks on colored people and the brilliantly wiseacre description of the Ulster situation in the chapter entitled "The Amusing Young Ladies of Down, the Fresh Young Ladies of Antrim, the Merry Young Ladies of Londonderry, the Coquettish Young Ladies of

Tyrone, Always So Amiable, the Smiling Young Ladies of Armagh, the Jolly Young Ladies of Fermanagh, Who Keep Those Very Beloved English Traditions, Come What May, in Ulster." The Celtic sense of black fun runs away with Cela in a number of places. He strips down to the last laugh which is savagely disguised by elaborate syntax and construction. In his almost piglike sense of a language-sty, all of this pun and games becomes glaringly reminiscent of Flann O'Brien. Belch laughters are babble-rousing, and curiously clear the air.

If Cela can't make you laugh, stay with the monkeys on Gibralter.

I would like to make comparisons with Irish writers. One thinks of Cela's *The Hive* and *Ulysses* as companion pieces of city design and detail, albeit the Irish comic belch is much louder. Cela is equally clever about messy human emotions, but Joyce brings more exuberance to their physical description. *Mrs. Caldwell Speaks to Her Son* reminds me of two other contemporary writers: Samuel Beckett and Desmond Hogan. The former is present in the reader's comprehension when the protagonist repeats statements and catalogs objects. Particularly towards the end, the novel shambles into a compulsive inventory like the vase in chapter 184 that breaks into a thousand pieces. Desmond Hogan, the most tantalizing of young Irish writers, often keeps the same breathless pace as Cela; his style, not yet entirely formed I think, drives like a whiz kid into people, places, and perceptions. There seems a gap between Cela and Irish writers in one respect. Dublin's fiction assumes that characters are based on actual people, while Cela's narratives, adventures, and fables primarily concern themselves, where it is necessary, with the construction of character from nothing. It is the difference between street and hothouse, between discovery and steam.

If critics find it difficult to deal with *Mrs. Caldwell Speaks to Her Son,* it must be because of their own crisis of metamorphoses of sensibility. The reader must remember this is a diary of fragments which assemble the dream body of a lost son. There is no letup in its author's concept of an erotic log that somehow the reader must assent to, if only in a state of sleep. One is not tired of most critical interpretations of the work, which are both Freudian and indispensable; it is that one wants more because more is there. As Yeats rightly whispers through the mask of Aherne:

> All dreams of the soul
> End in a beautiful man's or woman's body.

The Review of Contemporary Fiction (1984)

THREE

From McDaid's to Milwaukee: Brian Arkins Interviews James Liddy

ARKINS: You say you were educated by the monks of Glenstal and by Patrick Kavanagh in McDaid's. Could we start with the Benedictines – what did they teach you?

LIDDY: Rainer Maria Rilke has said that a Catholic childhood is a preparation for a mythical state of mind. I think this happened to me at the one Benedictine monastery in Ireland. I was given a sense of the aesthetic qualities of ritual, and of language. Beautiful Church Latin was sung by the monks and with it the possibility of the human voice in worshipping song.

The teaching of the Benedictines was a repetition of the founding European voice of St Benedict. This was echoed in the Milesian landscapes of Limerick. The glen with the Mass rock, the lake with the Anglo-Irish boathouse, trees and bushes brought by the Barringtons from all over the Empire, created a natural paradise for the supernatural songs. We walked for miles on the branches of the rhododendron bushes, like Mad Sweeney – under the direction of choreography of Kevin O'Nolan, the brother of Myles na gCopaleen. Visions, I think, often begin in extraordinarily glimpsed vistas.

An element in my education was my headmaster Matthew Dillon, the son of John Dillon, Land Leaguer and last leader of the Irish Parliamentary Party. Dom

Matthew poured into our ears the consciousness of a Catholic conservative nationalism that was wonderfully informed, but limited in scope. For instance, he would bellow at me for walking around the school with the *Collected Poems of W.B. Yeats* under my arm. Even then I knew that Yeats rode a winged horse while the monks rode nags – elegant nags, but still nags. Some of this high-flown, low-key, cultural nationalism has stayed with me. The Celtic millstone around the neck – not necessarily a wicked gift of a clerical godfather?

I'd like to say that the cadences of Church Latin in the choir at office, and the passionate utterance of classical Latin on the page, never leave one abandoned to them in youth. One is buried in them for life.

ARKINS: Let's move on to Kavanagh. It's true, I think, that he changed your life?

LIDDY: Let me say first about Kavanagh – and I have said a lot about him and written some – that before him I had only read, and read about, poets. Then I met one which is a very dangerous thing to do. It's like winning big at your first race meeting: you're hooked and that's definite. So I sat, for apparently wasted days and years, in the chapel of McDaid's learning the technique of breathing in what it is to be a poet; an exercise as casual as ordering another round for the master. This was Bohemia which is not an alternative university, but a world where verbal or other artistic gestures are done but not talked about. Ordinary existence gathered something when Kavanagh and his coterie sat at the bar or along the wall. Perhaps the Irish invented the alcoholic cafe; and perhaps if we take the model of French writing, the difference between French novelists and Irish poets is that the former actually work in the cafe, while the latter do their homework away from the scene.

Kavanagh would now and then, maybe like a church bell on the hour, say illuminating things. For instance, he would discuss Robert Frost in these terms, "The best and worst that can be said about Frost to me is this: They are competent, but they tell us nothing about God." This kind of statement was a very exciting addition to the voice of St. Benedict. It is a kind of modern cave voice of primitive religious apprehension; it scores the emotion of what I call a mythical mind. It stirs the power of word and idea association. And it brings in that other world of the ancestors. I find the same quality in Jack Kerouac's writing – I enjoy teaching a Kerouac and The Beat Generation course at the University of Wisconsin-Milwaukee. When Mike Wallace, on his show, asked Kerouac what he was after, that writer replied that he wanted to see God's face. I much prefer this pre-Christian, folk-Christian, image or epiphany to the solemnities of Eliot. Kavanagh discovered and brought the Beat poets into the attention of the British Isles. Kavanagh also liked the irreverent, cranky, poetics and wisdom of Ezra Pound. We need lots of this throw-away integrity now.

As anyone will agree who knows Kavanagh's poems, they are embedded with an archaic, but necessary feeling of love. A wide vibration of the sense of love shivers through his poetry. I think I have tried to catch this sideways feeling of Eros, agape, and gratitude in my work. The sense of being a messenger with obvious, but difficult news. And I do not believe the personal is political.

ARKINS: So Kavanagh launched you into poetry. Could you say something about your early work as a poet?

LIDDY: My early work as a poet seems now one of apprenticeship. I was learning my way through the strange disorder of my feelings. I was reading much poetry with a view of judging it, incorporating it, from the inside. My anxiety was that I would not have enough influence to sustain an independent journey. I wanted to be page-taught as well as life-taught. Read a poem once for emotion, once for intelligence, once for memory, and once to help your writing now.

Of course I was a middle-class child trying to wean myself out of that condition; poetry was a purple exit sign. I envied the roots of Kavanagh when I read and met him. I envied – and envy – the dark childhood of Thomas Kinsella which enabled him to harness such driving forces in his poems. When Belfast started burning, I envied also Padriac Fiacc who stayed there to watch the flames devour. I had to make my own way with a private life, travel, teaching and cafe attendance. My early poetry is obviously a nervous context which can sometimes prop a poem that might be good and readable. It was blessed, however, with a mountain, Croghan Kinsella, a region redolent in the bursting myths of Irish war and rhetoric, and an ancestral or genetic wildness. It is full of "Bless me, Father, for I have sinned." I hope it goes somewhere and leads somewhere. In putting together poems from this period for my anticipated *Collected Poems,* I thought my early work stayed better on the page than I had imagined. However, it was a fragile beginning, and I think I have built on it.

ARKINS: What, then, of your more recent poetry?

LIDDY: The recent work, which I think stretches back to the incoming of Baudelaire with his bar flowers out of poisonous cafes, has had many stages and preparations. I have worked in many different effervescences of my inherited and invented psyches; from translation to Tara burning bright or Kincora swinging low, to love poetry and the riddles and wisecracks of the inclement heart, to that tree of Tom Moore singing by the Avoca, which is the evocation of the English tradition in Irish writing

(English in language and in some nuances). Minor traditions in Irish and American literature have often been the most fruitful. I have been bold in making my connections. I have been swayed by distaste for the moral statement.

I really do not know if what I am saying has really anything to do with what I have been writing. Looking back though, it does seem that I have been attempting to cure certain deficiencies in Irish poetry that have opened in the last thirty years. The independent mind about cultural matters, which I think arises from Kavanagh, has performed as an anti-Siren for me. Also a sense of idealism relating to publication and publicity rituals has been significant to me.

Above all, I wished to restore humour and sarcasm to Irish poetry which was a feature of traditional Irish writing – something that is redolent of the 19th century.

Maybe I was amiss in always going directly ahead in writing, instead of taking time to try on different tones and textures. I have been basically impatient. But I was intrigued for a while by the dissociations of language that comes from the tradition of the French Symbolist and post-Symbolist poets. This surfaces now and then in my books. A more decisive matter, as some reviewers have pointed out, is the free verse expertise of American poetry, the sense of reality of language as it is. It is often forgotten that equally vital in American composition and process have been the significance of the local voice, whether New York, the West Coast, New England, the Mid-West, etc. I hope I have combined both the Irish and the American reliance on locality and place. A joint townland sound, maybe.

The main object in writing is to infuse your voice with what your furies, fairies, muses, want to say. Insist on saying. And I think in the new poems of *A White*

Thought in a White Shade I have commenced enforcing that obedience to the outside.

ARKINS: John Ashbery, the distinguished American poet has rated you "the most original among living Irish poets" and said you are superior to Heaney-Kinsella. How do you react to that?

LIDDY: I think Ashbery's comment is not as plain as that. It does put me in the context of Kinsella and Heaney, but, in my reading, it does not actually say "superior" in the sense of better. I think it uses the word in the sense of a similar or equal value. It can perhaps be construed either way, but let me take the modest path which is also the correct one.

I am very grateful for John Ashbery's comment and I wish him long life and the Nobel Prize. His first visit to Ireland was to the Gorey Arts Festival, and I have long been conscious of his stature as both a writer and a presence. I like his description of the process of poetry from his introduction to his friend Frank O'Hara's *Collected Poems,* "Trying on various pairs of brass knuckles until he finds the one which fits comfortably."

ARKINS: Creighton University Press has published your *Collected Poems.* I take it that was a big moment for you?

LIDDY: Certainly. It is the big moment. I am very grateful to Creighton University Press for this large undertaking. It will get the core of my work to the public. I was blessed with great publishers in my career: Liam Miller of the Dolmen Press and Graham Mackintosh of the White Rabbit Press in San Francisco and Santa Barbara. I believe I have been in the hands of the masters. Now Creighton University Press provides an ultimate cachet. I realize it will contribute to an understanding of my poetry, both in Ireland and America. I think it is a hopeful cultural sign that this kind of "twinning" takes place.

ARKINS: You have been teaching English for some time now at the University of Wisconsin-Milwaukee. How do you find that chimes with your writing of poetry?

LIDDY: I have been happily teaching creative writing, Irish literature and Beat literature for nearly twenty years at the University of Wisconsin-Milwaukee. I have been favored by my colleagues and my Department with extraordinary benevolent conditions of teaching. I have found my students in poetry-writing workshops to be in the main gifted, promising, and hardworking. There are differences in teaching graduate and undergraduate students, but I have had instructive and cordial ententes with both. I think their sure fire and enthusiasm helps my writing. The only problem is the question of time, for class and class preparation (not to mention office hours or even cafe hours) do take periods away from your work. But it is compensated for by the interaction with younger spirits.

Additionally, a poet does not work on the same schedule as a fiction writer. He or she can write at odd times and in odd places. The nucleus of a lot of good poetry is spontaneity, the sudden moment. Auden's poem on the novelist tells the story, and we poets are perhaps the lucky ones, in ways as free as the air.

The poet has a peculiar duty: he has to create other poets. We cannot let talent die without waking. Artists are the real born-againers.

ARKINS: What is your relationship to Ireland at this time? Is she the old sow that eats her farrow?

LIDDY: Joyce's metaphors were of course the response to the fake female and pastoral images of Pearse and the boys. Ms Ni Houlihan as a sow was the response to provocation. Yeats's nationalist image-kitty balances Joyce's though. And as we read the bible before we met literature, so we read Yeats before we understood modernism. So we are scorched or blasted into Irish consciousness, at least we were. I, too, have danced in Ireland, the Yeats reflection, and as a Catholic I have drunk from the holy wells (we know from Synge's *The Well of the Saints* how dangerous it is). The sense of ghosts and apparitions mixes ever with realism. My relationship to Ireland is dictated by the customary law of birth, exile, and possible return; it is the usual gathering of panic and confusion, complicated at the end of the century by the sudden loss in the culture of the sure sense of cyclic return. As a new 20th century nation we had almost too much identity, too certain of the curves of our psychic past - now as the result of academic revisionism and the permeation of a universal sex/drugs/rock and roll cocoon we are left with a diminishing local definition of ourselves. Yet the point of my witness and my rhythms lies between the points of return to somewhere and an expectation of arriving at nowhere. Recently I heard Archbishop Weakland of Milwaukee say in a homily, "I used not to take much notice of my Irish grandmother talking about spirits and ghosts, but there is something in it." I assent to that; in a sense artists here can still wear the diadem of the post-folkloric. But we are no longer certain of what the audience thinks.

ARKINS: It's no secret that you are gay. Do you regard that *as* an enabling factor in the writing of poetry?

LIDDY: What a delightful and inevitable question! We are in the midst of another nineties and the difference is between the love that dare not speak its name and the love that cannot stop speaking its name. I will have to say straightaway that being queer, like being Irish and being Catholic, has charted my imagination. Perhaps more than the other two, it takes or begs more space, being the most outwardly sensual. My dissent from the current realization of sexual liberation is that it seems to threaten the comic/creative sense. There is also value and depth in underground voltage. But much has been gained now for human dignity, "'tis a famous victory". And my life has to pursue its belated or blessed wickedness. As I wrote in a recent poem:

Can hope come from that
like from a hole in the ground?
Can we get that small
to become a seed?
Shaking out. Taking
whatever is our life
putting it on the ground.
Skin comes, what we admire
in people's bodies most of the time.
It is fun here. That's all, we
must learn to grow up,
we must have orgy
we must have heaven.
I ask every sentient being:
admire the lifestyle of
those who die and dream.

ARKINS: Your sexual poems are very powerful and you say in one, "I have the observance of the sexual life." Isn't that a very bold claim?

LIDDY: Boldness is all, there's nothing riper than boldness. Even if I whisper in a lower voice, I wish it had all worked out. But I won't go into my deprivation as compared with my expectation! An answer here would require reference to my poem "Dear Anima, Show These Words". The poem occurs at the moment of my mother's death. The soul is setting out on the waters from the West End rocks at Kilkee, a place she always loved. It has to swim into ocean purgation, while I have to go on with my life, which was conceived as a sensual adventure. My mother and I were everything, Princess and subject, muse and artist, mistress and servant, matriarch and rebel, each possible combination except audience and poet – but on one thing we were divided: I saw the open sexual life as an embodiment of love and purpose, and she traditionally saw it as salacious and rank. She defended monogamy, I adored (sometimes in moderation) the sybarite.

ARKINS: Another pervasive theme in your poems is an anti-romantic debunking of various Irish pieties. Could you comment on that?

LIDDY: Debunking of pieties – in a sense nothing is more pious or more required of the Irish artist. And here, like Allen Ginsberg, I have put my queer shoulder to the wheel. Let me quote you two poems:

Outside Lady Gregory's Garden
Carve your beloved names in mud.

Or

Remembering How They Stood
Where's the big house, Pat?
It's on the Lawrence collection, Sir.

Studies (1996)

NOTES

NOTES